Called to Equip

Called to Equip

*A Training and Resource Manual
for Pastors*

Palmer Becker

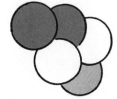

HERALD PRESS
Scottdale, Pennsylvania
Waterloo, Ontario

Library of Congress Cataloging-in-Publication Data
Becker, Palmer, 1936-
    Called to equip : a training and resource manual for pastors / Palmer
Becker.
        p.   cm.
    Includes bibliographical references.
    ISBN 0-8361-3623-3
    1. Church group work. 2. Small groups. 3. Lay ministry—Recruiting.
I. Title.
BV652.2.B43   1993
253'.7—dc20   93-12085
                                                                   CIP

CALLED TO EQUIP
Copyright © 1993 by Herald Press, Scottdale, Pa. 15683
    Published simultaneously in Canada by Herald Press,
    Waterloo, Ont. N2L 6H7. All rights reserved
Library of Congress Catalog Number: 93-12085
International Standard Book Number: 0-8361-3623-3
Printed in the United States of America
Book design by Gwen M. Stamm/Cover art by Joel Kauffman

1 2 3 4 5 6 7 8 9 10 00 99 98 97 96 95 94 93

*Dedicated to my colleagues
in the pastoral ministry*

Contents

Resources

Acknowledgments

I wish to acknowledge the help of Kenneth C. Haugk and the Stephen Ministries staff based in Saint Louis, Missouri, for many principles on which this Care Group ministry is based.

I am indebted to a host of persons who have sparked within me—and my wife, Ardys—a vision for Care Groups. Among these are Gordon Cosby, pastor of the Church of the Saviour (Washington, D.C.); Lyman Coleman, director of Serendipity House (Littleton, Colo.); Roberta Hestenes, president of Eastern Baptist Seminary (Philadelphia, Pa.); Carl F. George of the Fuller Institute (Pasadena, Calif.); and Melvin J. Steinbron, author of *Can the Pastor Do It Alone?*

Leonard Wiebe of Aurora, Colorado, helped us start small groups in our first church in Clinton, Oklahoma. Ed Goerzen, a seminary classmate, allowed me to watch as he effectively coordinated nearly fifty groups in the Willingdon Mennonite Brethren Church of Burnaby, B. C. Ed then helped us recruit, train, and supervise seventeen group leaders at the Peace Mennonite Church in Richmond, B. C. Our son, Byron, former participant in Assembly Mennonite Church (where small groups are central), offered continuing encouragement as these materials were being developed.

Introduction

The small group movement may be the best thing that has happened to the church since the Reformation. God is doing a new thing! In thousands of groups around the world, people are meeting God and each other in new ways. The Bible is becoming an open book. Hurting Christians are finding comfort and support. Growing Christians are finding new opportunities to minister. New Christians are entering the church.

Every renewal movement in church history has had roots in small groups. The early church began in people's homes, as did the Anabaptist, Wesleyan, and Pentecostal movements. The expansion of Christianity in South America, Africa, and Asia is largely due to small groups. Small groups are key to the new life being experienced in many North American churches.

I have a strong conviction that God is calling pastors to equip a new generation of lay pastors of small groups. If these lay leaders are well trained and filled with God's Spirit, there are few limits to what God can do through his people.

Buildings will not limit us because every home and conference room becomes a place for ministry. Staff will not limit us because lay people will do needed ministry. Finances will not limit us because small groups cost almost nothing.

God is opening new doors to our churches as he opened them to Moses in the wilderness or the apostles in the early church. There is no way we pastors alone can meet all the needs and opportunities for ministry in a local congregation. Moses tried it and his father-in-law advised, "What you are doing is not good!" (Exod. 18:17).

Moses was wearing himself out doing too much. This was good neither for him nor the people. They were waiting in line yet still not getting their needs met. It was not good for potential leaders. Their gifts were neither being developed nor used.

On Jethro's advice, Moses asked his congregation to choose leaders with whom he could work. They chose leaders and organized into small groups of ten where their basic needs could be met. Moses remained responsible for the overall leadership and ministry of the people but now he did the work of ministry together with a team of lay pastors.

Called to Equip is a step-by-step manual for pastors who want to develop a team of persons with and through whom they can do ministry. If you are such a pastor, these materials will help you recruit, train, commission, supervise, and affirm a team of small group leaders. Through group leaders you can minister to the needs of your people and the people of your community. This manual asks and responds to twenty-six questions that will help you address concerns often raised concerning beginning and maintaining small group ministry.

Small groups, which in this manual will be called Care Groups, are seen as an answer to two key questions: "How can we meet the needs of the people that we have?" and "How can we reach those that we do not yet have?"

Called to Equip presents a philosophy of ministry in which Care Groups led by trained, supervised leaders become the key pastoral and evangelistic structure of the church. Pastors will grow close to their lay leaders as they equip and encourage their ministry.

A companion guide, *Called to Care*, is a manual for Care

Group leaders. Persons interested in developing a ministry team will want to read both manuals carefully before seeking to begin a Care Group ministry.

A Care Group includes five to twelve persons who have gathered around a common interest or need. They meet regularly at a time and place convenient to the members. At the meetings, members experience informal fellowship, Bible study in dialogue form, sharing, personal support, and prayer.

Most groups are open and will seek to invite new persons to join them. Groups are voluntary. No one will be "put" into a group. But in time, it is hoped that every attender of your congregation will be invited to become part of a suitable Care Group and that 60, 80, or even 90 percent of the attenders will voluntarily choose to respond to the invitation.

Thirty years ago Robert E. Coleman wrote a classic guide, *The Master Plan of Evangelism*.[1] It outlined the master plan of Jesus, who selected twelve disciples, associated with them, taught them, and modeled ministry for them. He delegated responsibility to them, supervised them, then watched them reproduce. These materials are built on that master plan of Jesus.

Some may find this manual overwhelming. Let me quickly say you don't have to follow all suggestions to initiate small group ministry. A small group can begin whenever you and two or three others agree to meet regularly in Christ's name.

If a ministry is to expand and be a ministry of excellence, it needs to be done decently and in order. If Care Groups are worth doing, they are worth doing well! It is with that in mind that these resources have been developed. When used carefully, they will help you to develop a Care Group ministry of excellence that will be an honor to God.

—Palmer Becker
Mountain Lake, Minnesota

Called to Equip

1 Planting a Vision

What Is Your Vision?

What is your vision for the church? What should the church be? How are you going to get there? These are basic questions we pastors need to ask. They give perspective and focus to our work.

No one can give a vision to another person. Each of us needs to capture the vision that is right for our setting. We can learn from the visions of others, but to be effective, a vision needs to be something we can feel in our hearts and picture in our minds for our situation.

Reading biblical passages and books can be helpful. You might begin with Exodus 18:7-26; Mark 10:35-45; Matthew 28:16-20; Acts 6:1-7; 1 Timothy 3:1-7, and 2 Timothy 2:2. Books on small groups such as *20/20 Vision* by Dale Galloway[2] or *Successful Home Cell Groups* by Paul Yonggi Cho[3] are also helpful.

The church is to be a friendly, caring community. We are to be an accepting, forgiving family of people who care for each other. We want to show compassion for each other and the people in our wider world. What vision do you have for helping your congregation become a caring congregation where needs are met?

People go to where their needs are met. They go home at the end of the day when they need rest, food, and love. They go to school when they need information or skills. Why are people coming—or not coming—to your church or mine? Generally caring congregations do not have attendance problems.

Throughout history God has met the needs of his people in both large and small settings. That was true with Moses and the Hebrew people in the wilderness. It was true of Jesus who preached to thousands but also had his group of twelve. Whenever the church has experienced renewal, there has been a healthy balance of ministry in both large and small groupings.

No pastor, not even a team of pastors, can listen to and effectively care for each person in a congregation. There are too many joys, too many opportunities, stresses, conflicts, and pressures. There is not enough time to personally care for each attender and also preach good sermons, teach effective classes, and attend to administrative details.

Visions for offering pastoral care often rotate around three basic patterns. The three visions for offering ministry may be diagramed as follows.

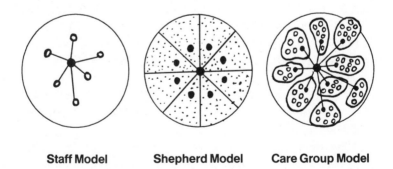

Staff Model   **Shepherd Model**   **Care Group Model**

The first and most common of the models is the **Staff Model.** In this model pastors say, "We'll do it." They minister to the congregation through worship, teaching, and counseling. They may recruit and train assistants, deacons, and helpers to assist in ministering to those who are in special need. This pattern has been well developed in the Stephen Ministries program directed by Kenneth C. Haugk. The plan is good but generally fails to provide personal, week-by-week pastoral care to the majority of attenders.

A second vision for pastoral care is the **Shepherd Model.** In this model, families of the congregation are divided geographically or in some other manner among deacons or shepherds of the church. Shepherds seek to meet individually with each family once a year or as needed. Melvin J. Steinbron has described this model well in his book, *Can the Pastor Do it Alone?*

This model is also effective, but it does not adequately take into account the voluntary and community nature of the church. Members often feel resistant to being assigned to a shepherd or shepherd group. And since such groups do not meet weekly, regular needs of members are often not noticed.

These materials propose a third model. It is the **Care Group Model**, in which **Care Groups become the key pastoral structure of the church.** This model affirms that the church is a voluntary, caring community of believers who seek to meet the personal and spiritual needs of each other and those they are called to reach. Dale E. Galloway pioneered an approach to this model in his book, *20/20 Vision.*

In Care Groups Christians can corporately function as a close-knit family of brothers and sisters. They pray for each other by name, discuss with each other what the Bible means for them, and are available to each other in times of need. This kind of caring usually happens best in small groups of twelve or fewer.

These materials present a vision for a congregation of small groups led by lay pastors. What model is best for your congregation? I invite you to read this manual and give serious consideration to the Care Group Model. In some situations, a combination of the three visions or models for ministry may be needed.

How Will You Share Your Vision?

If you have a vision for Care Groups in your church, how will you bring your church on board? What is your plan for sharing the vision? Here are four suggestions.

1. Preach your vision. God gave visions to the prophets and to the apostles. They preached them. You can do the same. John Maxwell preached a series called "Small Groups Make a Big Difference": (1) They Help the Pastor, (2) They Help the People, (3) They Help the Purpose. (Tapes with outlines are available from Injoy Ministries, PO Box 828, Bonita, CA 92002. Other outlines are given in LIFE Curriculum Guide III, PO Box 1245, Elkhart, IN 46517.)

If you preach a sermon or a series of sermons, consider a testimony or a series of testimonies on those Sundays. Ask people to share who have been ministered to in small groups.

2. Experience your vision. Care Groups are relational. Relationships need to be experienced, not only talked about. If you have not experienced a Care Group, visit a group in your church or in another. If your potential leaders have not experienced a group, offer to lead one. This manual (and its companion, *Called to Care)* will tell you how.

You might also introduce elements of Care Group life in a deacon or other meeting. Begin your meeting by asking a sharing question at the beginning or praying for each other by name. Minister to each other before you talk about ministering to others. *Called to Care* will help you get started.

John Mallison says, "Once people have experienced the depth of care, concern, and growth possible in a vital small group, they will generally never again be completely satisfied with trying to be a Christian alone." [4]

3. Visualize your vision. We live in a visual age. Diagram your present model for ministry. Does it resemble a staff, shepherd, or Care Group model? Analyze who is or is not being ministered to. Take the diagram to your church board. Debate the three traditional models for offering ministry. Which is best for you and your church?

To help your congregation visualize groups, model a small group for everyone to see. Model a group in a "fishbowl" illustration during a Sunday morning or evening service in September. Use posters, pictures, and audiovisuals that will help the congregation visualize a caring church.

4. Discuss, shape, and recommend your vision. Resource 1 (below) outlines possible objectives, assumptions, and guidelines for a Care Group ministry. Develop an outline of your own.

Call together a task group of several persons from the congregation that you feel would be open and supportive to the idea of Care Groups.

Discuss your vision with them and let them shape or modify the guidelines. Ask such questions as, "When you think of small groups, what comes to mind?" "Why should we have groups?" "Why shouldn't we?" "How would groups form?" After developing a list of possible objectives, assumptions, and guidelines, take them as a recommendation to your church board for discussion and affirmation in principle.

Resource 2 is a sample brochure for introducing groups to the congregation. You might modify it for your congregation. Also have available possible materials that might be used for study in the groups. A brochure and materials can help define the different types of groups. Most people reject groups because no option meets their needs. People go to where their needs are being met!

What Might Be Objections?

Care Groups are not for everyone. What objections might you encounter? Let's respond to five.

1. "Groups would weaken our Sunday school program." Although some have only one or the other, most churches can have both a strong Sunday school and a strong Care Group program. Sunday school emphasizes content while Care Groups focus on people and experience.

Some Sunday school classes are able to function as Care Groups. They begin with personal sharing and prayer for each member. If this is true, invite leaders of Sunday school classes to take the model training outlined in *Called to Care*. If they take the training and want their classes to become Care Groups, invite them to become part of the monthly supervisory meetings as outlined in chapter 6.

However, there is usually a big difference between a study class and a Care Group. Sunday school class periods are usually too short for the fellowship and sharing desired in a Care Group. If members are not sharing personal concerns or praying for each other in their Sunday school classes, these classes should not be misrepresented as Care Groups. (See Part II in *Called to Care* for the basic elements of a Care Group.)

2. "Groups would weaken our families." Strong families should be encouraged. Members of a close family should study the Bible, pray for each other, share their feelings, and care deeply for one another! In fact, each family should be encouraged to function as a miniature church or Care Group. Parents need to be primary caregivers.

But sometimes families are not functioning properly and that is precisely why family members need a Care Group. A Care Group can help members be the kind of parents or family members they are meant to be. Encourage people who believe in family to try a Care Group for eight weeks. A Care Group can make family even better.

3. "Groups would take time from my other responsibilities."

Committees are important but the aim should be to move from committee to community. A committee meeting can begin with personal resourcing, the sharing of personal needs, and prayer. Committee members should minister to each other before they talk about ministering to others. When such ministry within a group is happening, encourage committee members to see their committee as a Care Group. Invite the chairperson to take training and function as a Care Group leader.

But note that much committee work can be done through Care Groups. Care Groups can organize socials, projects, and special seminars on behalf of the church. They can even lead worship or elements in it. When Care Groups are the key pastoral structure of the church, some committees will become unnecessary. (See chapter 4 in *Called to Care* for ideas on how committees can be helped to function as mission groups.)

4. "Groups sometimes become devisive or cliquish." These training materials address the key problems that churches have experienced in relationship to groups. Lack of supervision has caused some groups to become schismatic, divisive, and cliquish. (These concerns and others are spoken to in Part III of *Called to Care*. Also see Resource 3, Questions and Answers About Care Groups at the end of this chapter).

5. "We don't have anyone to lead groups." God always provides the gifts and resources needed for his work in a congregation. Chapter 2 of this manual and Resource 5, Potential Care Group Leaders, will assist you in the recruitment process.

Resource 4, Suggested Job Descriptions, will help your interested people or church board to capture a vision concerning who and how people will be involved. Job descriptions have a way of giving content to vision. They give people necessary information, security, and guidance. But they also make the requirements specific and often lead to considerable discussion. Do not introduce them too early in the discussion.

Summary Checklist for Planting a Vision

Each chapter in this manual will end with a step-by-step summary checklist you might want to use to plan your calendar or to monitor your progress towards establishing a Care Group ministry in your church. Following is a checklist for phase one—planting a vision.

____**Step 1: Read and pray**.

Read and study suggested biblical passages and books. Seek to capture the vision that God has for you and your church. Spend time in prayer and personal retreat seeking a philosophy of ministry that will provide compassionate care and leadership for each person in your congregation.

____**Step 2: Preach a sermon or teach a class on caregiving**.

Preaching inspires, encourages, and brings people to commitment. Preach a sermon or a series of sermons on our caring God. Clarify that your responsibilities as pastor are to see to it that the people are ministered to rather than to personally do it all. For a class consider using the text *Christian, Caregiving: A Way of Life,* by Kenneth C. Haughk (Minneapolis, Minn.: Augsburg Publishing House, 1984). (Teaching outlines for the book are available from LIFE, Box 347, Elkhart, IN 46517.)

____**Step 3: Bring a recommendation to your church board**.

Outline your vision. Allow key people in the church to help you shape it. Then bring a recommendation and share your heart with your board. Ask them to help you find a way to adequately minister to all persons in the congregation. See Resources 1 and 2 for assistance. Help your board to understand the ministry and adopt a set of guidelines.

____Step 4: Keep the congregation informed.
Keep the congregation informed concerning the unfolding ministry. Write articles for your newsletter. Announce a training program. Ask persons in a small group to share what a small group has meant in their life. You might want to prepare a brochure or poster to help share the vision. See Resources 2 and 3. Be prepared to respond to objections in a nondefensive manner.

RESOURCE 1

Possible Objectives, Assumptions, and Guidelines for a Care Group Ministry

A. Basic Objective

The purpose of a Care Group ministry is to make it possible for each person in the congregation—and eventually in the community—to experience regularly and personally the caring, forgiving, and purposeful love of Jesus Christ.

B. Basic Assumptions

1. Our God who lives in community wants each of his children to experience as well the richness of life in community. The church is to be an inviting, forgiving, and reconciling community.

2. Personal care and a sense of community often happen best in small groups of twelve or less. Care Groups are different from most Sunday school classes or committees.

3. Caring groups have magnetic healing and evangelistic powers. People go to where their needs are being met.

4. With proper training and supervision, lay caregivers are able and often eager to offer pastoral care to a small group of people.

C. Basic Guidelines

1. The pastor or an overall coordinator, under guidance of the church board, will give direction to the Care Group ministry.

2. Care Group leaders will be recruited, trained, commissioned, and guided to excellence. Supervision and continuing education will be offered.

3. Leaders will each choose an apprentice so there will be a built-in pattern for sharing leadership and beginning new groups. Some leaders may serve as facilitators who share leadership functions with other members of the group.

4. All members and new attenders of the congregation will be invited to be part of a Care Group. In most instances, the Care Group leaders under guidance of the pastor will do the inviting.

5. Most groups will be open. They will practice the "empty

chair principle," which challenges the group to think of a new person or couple that could benefit from the group.

6. Most groups will meet once a week and not less than twice a month. They will meet regularly at a time and place most convenient to the group.

7. Care Group leaders will meet together with the pastor monthly for encouragement, peer supervision, and in-service training. Attendance is required.

8. The pastor or overall coordinator will meet one-on-one with individual group leaders as needed and will occasionally visit the Care Group meetings.

9. Depending on the level of care that they seek to offer, persons who represent Sunday school classes, youth groups, and committees may be part of the Care Group leaders' meetings.

Sample Care Groups Brochure

CARE GROUPS

The Key to

CLOSE

ACCEPTING

RELATIONSHIPS

At

**Bethel Mennonite Church
301 N 9th Street
Mountain Lake, MN 56159
507 427-3075**

(Panel 1)

Our Basic Assumptions

1. Our God is a caring God who wants us to know the richness and support of a caring community.

2. The church is a caring community that offers close, accepting relationships through careful listening, forgiving attitudes, and personal care.

3. Personal care and community become most concrete and meaningful in small groups of twelve or less. We call these Care Groups.

4. Care Groups are becoming the key pastoral structure of our church. Care Group leaders are trained and supervised by our pastors and become part of the pastoral team.

5. The pastoral team invites all attenders to become part of a Care Group. The second and fourth Sunday evenings of the month are left unscheduled as one possible time for these groups to meet.

"God has so arranged the body . . . that . . . the members may have the same care for one another. If one member suffers, all suffer together . . . if one member is honored, all rejoice together" (1 Cor. 12:24-26, NRSV).

(Panel 2)

Qualities of a Care Group

- Has five to twelve members.

- Comes together around a common interest or need.

- Meets regularly (weekly, biweekly, monthly) at a time and place most convenient to its members.

- Is people-centered. Meetings are filled with fellowship, study, and dialogue.

- Groups agree to confidentiality. Nobody criticizes behind another's back.

- Group members listen to and care for each other. They pray for each other and help each other in times of need.

- Group leaders meet with each other and the pastor monthly for supervision and continuing education.

AN INVITATION
You are warmly invited to begin or join a Care Group sponsored by Bethel Church. See back for options.

(Panel 3)

My Response

Yes! I want to be part of a Care Group that meets:

____Weekly. Suggest time: _____

____On second and fourth Sunday evenings.

____Monthly. Suggest time: _____

The type of group I would prefer is:

____**Nurture Group**—It has a balance of fellowship, sharing, study, and prayer. Options for study might include the Parables or Gospel of Mark.

____**Support Group**—It focuses on a special personal need. Options might include parenting, marriage enrichment, grief/loss/divorce recovery, and compassion fatigue.

____**Evangelistic Group**—Unchurched people make up half the group.

____**Mission Group**—The group will focus on a special social, program, or community need.

I would enjoy being in a group with:

_____ as leader.

_____ a trusted friend.

_____ a new person.

Name _____ Tel _____

(Panel 4)

31

RESOURCE 3

Questions and Answers About Care Groups
For use by pastors to interpret Care Groups
to the congregation

Our church is exploring the possibility of beginning Care
Groups. Following are questions and answers to help us in our
understanding and discussion.

What is a Care Group?
It has three to twelve members.
Members come together around a common interest or need.
They meet weekly, biweekly, or monthly in homes.
They include Bible study, dialogue, prayer, and fellowship.

Who needs one?
People who want to grow in their Christian life.
Everyone needs a group of some kind. We hope to offer a
wide variety.
Some need a nurture group while others need a mission or
support group.
Groups are voluntary. No one will be coerced into being part
of a group.
Care Groups meet for a set period and then decide about
continuing.
Seekers are welcomed and encouraged to see what the
Christian life is about.

Who will lead Care Groups?
Training classes will be held for potential group leaders in
which they will be trained in leading small group dialogue.
Care Groups may choose their own leaders or facilitators. But
for the sake of unity and good care, these leaders must attend
monthly meetings for mutual supervision and continuing education.

What kind of a commitment will you need to make?

To meet regularly. If you need to be absent, call.

To be confidential and to not criticize behind another's back.

To pray for each other and to be available in time of need.

What are our basic assumptions about Care Groups?

That our God is a caring God who wants us to experience a friendly, caring community.

That the church is to be a sharing, forgiving, reconciling community.

That such a community becomes most concrete in small groups of twelve or less.

That Care Groups can be the key pastoral and evangelistic structure of the church.

That lay leaders are willing and able to provide basic pastoral care to a small group.

That every attender will be invited to a group but that no one will be "put" into a group.

What if I have further questions?

For more information call _____

RESOURCE 4

Suggested Job Descriptions

1. The church board
a. Is responsible to the membership for establishing the general objectives and guidelines for the Care Group ministry. (See Resource 1 for suggestions.)

b. Is responsible for clarifying a job description for the pastor or overall coordinator who will lead the Care Group ministry in an efficient and effective manner.

2. The pastor or overall coordinator
a. Is responsible under guidance of the church board/council for the pastoral care of the congregation.

b. Is responsible for recruiting, training, and supervising a team of Care Group leaders who will assist in giving pastoral care to all who attend the church.

c. Will assist Care Group leaders and the church in the formation and growth of small groups.

d. Details of responsibility will include:
- Communicating a vision for Care Groups to the church.
- Recruiting qualified Care Group leaders.
- Training Care Group leaders by leading a one-day retreat (or by leading a model Care Group as described in *Called to Care*).
- Recommending qualified, trained Care Group leaders to the church board for commissioning.
- Leading the commissioning service.
- Leading monthly meetings of the Care Group leaders for the purpose of offering encouragement, supervision, and continuing education.
- Meeting one-on-one with each leader to help select study materials, to deal with difficult situations, and to mentor personal and spiritual growth.
- Praying by name at least weekly for each Care Group leader.

- Reporting regularly to the church board so it can assess, affirm, and guide the ministry.

3. A Care Group leader

a. Is responsible for recruiting three to twelve persons to form a group.

b. Is responsible to the pastor for the week-to-week pastoral care of the persons in his or her Care Group.

c. Is responsible for modeling Christian discipleship and for maintaining his or her personal spiritual growth.

d. Details of responsibility will include:

- Fostering a climate of acceptance and mutual care in the group.
- Helping the group to agree on a covenant which will include the purpose of the group, meeting time, materials to be used.
- Ministering to individuals in the group as needed.
- Praying by name at least weekly for each group member.
- Delegating to individual group members such responsibilities as hosting, leading music, occasionally leading the study, planning a retreat, exploring a service project.
- Leading the group in a way which encourages all members to contribute their thoughts, feelings, and gifts.
- Timing the group meetings so that there is an effective and balanced emphasis on fellowship, Bible study, worship, and mission.
- Assisting in the training of an apprentice to the point where he or she is capable of leading a new group or of leading the present group so the original leader can begin a new group.
- Referring to the pastor or a trained counselor those members who are in need of professional counseling or care.
- Helping each member develop a positive regard for the church and its leadership.
- Attending monthly meetings of the Care Group leaders for peer supervision and continuing education.

2 Recruiting Leaders

How Many Leaders Do You Need?

A bell curve can be used to describe the involvement of people in a local church. The curve for the average local church looks something like the following:

Involvement in church

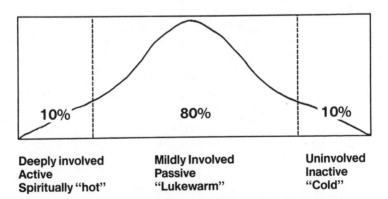

10%	80%	10%
Deeply involved	**Mildly Involved**	**Uninvolved**
Active	**Passive**	**Inactive**
Spiritually "hot"	**"Lukewarm"**	**"Cold"**

Peter Wiwcharuck in *Building Effective Leadership* analyzes the above by pointing out that the 10 percent shown as "active" are basically those who have been hired or elected to leadership positions. Instead of activating the potential 80 percent force, these leaders usually do the work themselves. The 80 percent who are passive remain inactive or mildly involved because there is basically nothing for them to do other than attend meetings.[5] Leaders need to help the 80 percent become ministry-oriented so that they can be doers of the word and persons who reach out to the uninvolved.

"One of the greatest responsibilities of leadership is people development," says Wiwcharuck. "Unfortunately, church leaders are often so busy doing things for people that they fail to develop the potential that God has placed in the church. The power of the church is in the doers." [6] The apostle James challenges all members to be "doers of the word and not hearers only."

To activate the mildly involved 80 percent for ministry, 10-15 percent of the congregation needs to be involved in a people-development kind of leadership. A bell curve showing this ratio looks as follows:

Leader to worker ratio

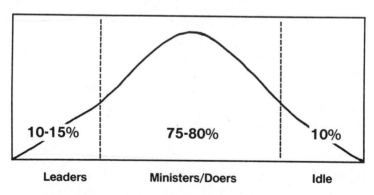

10-15%	75-80%	10%
Leaders	**Ministers/Doers**	**Idle**

In the classic story of Jethro and Moses, Moses the leader was doing all the work. He was wearing himself out. Jethro advised, "Choose some capable men and appoint them as leaders of the people: leaders of thousands, hundreds, fifties, and tens. They must be God-fearing men who can be trusted and who cannot be bribed." [7]

Busy, hurried pastors are not necessarily good pastors. The evidence of being a good pastor is not in the effort but in how many people are actually receiving effective ministry.

These materials will help you choose a team of Care Group leaders to help you get the job done! While you need to be a doer of ministry, the greater challenge is for you to minister with and through a team of qualified Care Group leaders. You are to be a leader of leaders. In this way your effectiveness can be multiplied and you can be spared burn-out.

Delegation of ministry will not reduce the overall weight of the responsibility you carry. By choosing a team of Care Group leaders, you are not passing the buck to others! You will still be accountable to your church to see that all people attending the congregation receive ministry. But you are exchanging the weight of direct ministry for the weight of ministering to and through team members.

Resource 5, Potential Care Group Leaders is a tool to help you choose from your congregation one leader per twelve regular attenders. Instructions will be given later in this manual to help you choose potential leaders who are hospitable, respected, sensitive, motivated, and firmly grounded.

It might be better to start small. It is better to start with one or two group leaders rather than not to start at all. Meeting with two or three lay persons for thirteen weeks in a model Care Group can be a rewarding experience! Choosing one leader per twelve may be phase two.

What Qualities Must Care Group Leaders Have?

Leaders of ministry need to evidence the qualities listed in the beatitudes of Jesus or the list Paul outlines in Galatians 5:22. As you choose leaders, remember that:

Leadership is not position. Position gives authority to people. Unfortunately some would-be leaders want authority without shouldering the responsibilities of a servant. Jesus pointed out that while certain scribes and Pharisees were filling leadership positions, they were not true leaders as he defined leadership. Leaders must have a heart for ministry (see Matt. 23:1-12).

Leadership is not personality. A charismatic personality gives people influence. Unfortunately some persons have influence or charisma but are not adequately qualified, trained, or appointed to positions of leadership. Ministry people want to serve others, not impress them with their personality or style.

Leadership is not management. Management has to do with ideas, organization, and policy. These are essential but leadership has to do with people. When leadership people move up to management, they often stop doing direct ministry work. Group leaders need to be people-oriented.

Christian leadership is servanthood, not lordship. Human beings corrupted by sin tend to seek dominion over everything in reach. Jesus teaches us that to be of great influence we need to be servants. Servants focus on meeting the needs of people and helping them reach their goals. While leading they ask, "Whose needs are being met—my needs or the needs of people I lead?"

Christian leaders are servants eager to learn everything they can about their group members. Then they help them to set and reach godly objectives within their capabilities. Leaders help their people make decisions, solve problems, and develop their qualities so God's worthwhile and just goals can be met.

Essential qualities for Christian leaders according to 1 Timothy 3 can be summarized as:

    1. Hospitable—Christian leaders are warm and friendly. They are known for their love. (John 13:35.)

2. **Respected**—They are people of integrity. They are
   committed to God and trusted by family and friends.
   (1 Timothy 3:1-7.)
3. **Sensitive**—They actively listen and have good relational skills. They are gifted with the spirit and more
   concerned about others than themselves. (Acts 6:1-7.)
4. **Motivated**—They are enthused about their faith,
   group, and church. They communicate enthusiasm to
   others. (1 Peter 5:1-7.)
5. **Grounded**—They know Scripture and are firmly committed to Christ and the church. (Acts 20:27-32.)

Whom Will You Ask?

A church needs leaders for both its organization and its or-
ganism. Those who have natural ability to manage finances, facilities, and organization should be affirmed for these needed
tasks. The first deacons or finance committee described in Acts
6 were chosen to do the details or organization so the apostles
could have time to preach, teach, and pray.

Which people in your church need to be released for direct
ministry to people? How can they be identified and recruited?

Take the attenders list of your congregation. Go through
the list name by name, seeking individuals and couples who
are hospitable, respected, sensitive, motivated, and grounded.
List persons regardless of present positions being held. Consider both men and women. In couples, underline the partner
most qualified to lead. Pray God will give you unselfish and
wise discernment. You may want to work on this task with a
team of trusted elders (Resource 5 will help).

Handpicking Care Group leaders in this way has the advan-
tage that you get whom you want. You need not deal with un-
qualified volunteers. But there are disadvantages. You may
miss gifted people. People not asked may have hurt feelings.
And not going public with the invitation works against build-

ing ownership and support in the entire congregation. It may even lead to some individuals feeling that the Care Group ministry is the pastor's pet project or a society either for the elite or the maladjusted.

In addition to handpicking recruits, extend an open invitation to all members of the congregation to enter the Care Group leader training program. This opens the possibility of discovering gifted people you might never have thought to ask. People will know that this program is open to them whenever they are free to participate in it. Offering the program may uncover willing people who may not be qualified to lead a Care Group but would be suitable for other ministries.

Consider publicizing the recruitment process through bulletin announcements, a poster, and newsletter articles. Publicly announce the training group during the worship service or in new membership and adult education classes. Resource 6, Invitations to Leadership Training, contains several possibilities.

How Do You Ask?

Jesus was direct in asking his first disciples to follow him. "Follow me," he said. "I will make you fishers of men." In the same way, single out and give a clear challenge to the persons you have identified for becoming Care Group leaders. Invite them as a group to your house for an evening of discussion and brainstorming.

Be enthusiastic and properly assertive as you challenge the potential Care Group leaders to come to the group meeting. Do not ask, "Would you be interested in being a Care Group leader?" That does not adequately communicate your enthusiasm for the program nor affirm the potential you see in the person.

Do not say, "We need ten people like you who have gifts for leading Care Groups. Would you be willing to sign up?" This seeks to fill slots rather than affirm gifts. Such a request may cause guilt and apply pressure. It may overlook some crises or issue in timing that the person may be facing.

Rather say, "I would like to invite you to work with me as a Care Group leader. From what I know about you, you have the qualities needed. And I believe you would benefit greatly from the training program."

You might want to extend the invitation by letter, then confirm it with a telephone conversation. Seek a firm commitment from each person to come to the meeting of potential leaders. Give the person time to think and pray about the challenge.

When your potential Care Group leaders gather, share your vision for a ministry-oriented church filled with friendly, caring people. Do this by reviewing together with possible leaders the brochure or objectives sheet you prepared earlier to introduce the program to the church or church board. Make modifications as needed. Share a job description with them. Again be prepared to make necessary changes. (See Resources 1 to 4 at the end of chapter 1.)

Set a definite time for the beginning of a training program. Resources 7 and 8 will help introduce the best training program for you.

If you open the training program to all persons interested in the church, it is important to have a personal interview with each potential Care Group leader at the end of the training period. Jesus had more than seventy disciples but from among them chose twelve to give crucial leadership (see Luke 6:12-14). In preparation for commissioning, Resource 10, Interview with Potential Care Group Leader, suggests questions and topics for discussion.

Summary Checklist for Recruiting Leaders
____Step 1: Decide how many leaders you need.

If you want to invite each attender of your church to a Care Group, seek to recruit one person for every twelve attenders. If you choose to begin small, choose several persons who might join you in being part of a model Care Group. Lyman Coleman in *Prologue to Small Groups* says, "One person with a genuine hunger is enough to start a group. One group is enough to penetrate a community. The question is not one of quantity, but quality." [8]

____**Step 2: Determine qualities you will look for in leaders.**
Look for persons who are hospitable, respected, sensitive, motivated, and grounded. Study 1 Timothy 3:1-13. Complete Resource 5, Potential Care Group Leaders.

____**Step 3: Invite potential leaders to an informal meeting.**
Discuss your vision, objectives, assumptions, and guidelines. Outline a training program, establish a specific starting date, and invite their participation.

____**Step 4: Publicly announce the training sessions.**
Announce the training program in the church bulletin and other appropriate ways (see Resource 6). Clarify that not all persons who take the training will automatically become leaders. Persons not interested in or suitable for leading a group will be helped to find an appropriate place for service.

Potential Care Group Leaders

NAME QUALITIES PREVIOUS EXPERIENCE

	Hospitable	Respected	Sensitive	Motivated	Grounded	

RESOURCE 6

Invitations to Leadership Training

A. Possible Bulletin Announcement

The church board would like to invite members with a heart for ministry to consider becoming Care Group leaders. A model Care Group **[or a day of orientation]** led by Pastor _____ will begin **[date and place].** Care Group leaders will be helped to recruit a small group of persons and facilitate regular meetings for the purpose of fellowship, study, prayer, and sharing. For more information, contact the office or any board member.

B. Possible Poster

BE A CAREGIVER!

LEARN HOW TO
- **Lead a Bible study**
- **Listen to hurting people**
- **Care for each other in a group**

[day of week, time, place]

For more information call: [name or place, number]

C. Possible Letter of Invitation

Dear

Greetings in the name of the One who cares most deeply.

At various times and in different places, we have been talking about beginning Care Groups at _____ Church. You have been nominated as a person we believe has insights and qualities that could be helpful in this ministry. I invite you (and your spouse) to our house for a time of discussion and brainstorming in regard to Care Groups. Could you come at _____ on _____?

We will explore what comes to mind when we think of small groups and why we should or should not have Care Groups. If we began Care Groups, how would the groups be formed? When would training be offered?

I will confirm this invitation by phone. An evening together would be a delight. I hope it will be of mutual benefit.

Love in Christ,

3 Training Leaders

Why Train Leaders?

Leadership is essential. Without adequate leadership, a Care Group is doomed. With quality leadership Care Group members can have a profitable experience and their needs can be met by persons competent for the task.

We are under orders by Jesus not only to make disciples but to teach them the content and skills we have learned. Leadership is learned. It is not so much a natural ability as something we make happen.

There is no such thing as a leaderless group. If an assigned leader fails to lead, the most talkative or influential person in the group will take charge. Leadership is influence and influence is everything!

Without trained leaders, many needs in the congregation will not be met. A pastor alone cannot meet all needs. The goal of a Care Group ministry is to provide a lay pastor for every member of the congregation!

Servant leaders are key to a healthy group and congregation. Group members generally go as far as trusted leaders lead or allow them to go. Poor group leaders tend to take their people only as far as they themselves are able or willing to go. A good group leader, regardless of personal limitations, focuses on needs of the group and seeks to help members develop their potential so the individuals and group can move forward.[9]

How Are Care Group Leaders Trained?

Research indicates that after thirty days people remember 10 percent of what they hear, 50 percent of what they see, 70 percent of what they say, and 90 percent of what they do.[10] Students do what they see, not what they hear. With this in mind, four basic steps will provide a conceptual framework for the learning process.

> Step 1: "I do, you watch."
> Step 2: "I do, you assist."
> Step 3: "You do, I assist."
> Step 4: "You do, I watch."

As pastor, or overall coordinator, you will begin the training of potential leaders by modeling a Care Group. This may be done either in a one-day concentrated seminar or through mentoring potential leaders in a twelve-week model Care Group. Resource 7, Leadership Training Seminar, outlines the concentrated seminar. Resource 8, Twelve-Week Model Training Group, outlines the model training group experience. Feel free to make copies of these outlines for discussion with your potential leaders.

A twelve-week experience is recommended. It gives each participant an opportunity to lead and allows needed time to integrate the learnings.

If you follow the twelve-week model, plan to spend two hours together each week. A suggested schedule for an evening might look as follows.

7:30-8:00	Welcome and opening sharing question
8:00-8:45	Bible study using a dialogue form
8:45-9:00	Personal sharing and prayer
9:00-9:20	Study one chapter from *Called to Care,* which will also help you apply your group experience and teach a basic principle or skill
9:20-9:30	Closing and refreshments

Actually, a model Care Group meeting will be like any other Care Group meeting except that it will end with the twenty-minute teaching and application session. (See 9:00-9:20 in the above schedule.) Each week after the Bible study, you will teach one chapter from *Called to Care* and help the group evaluate that day's meeting by using the application exercise at the end of that chapter.

For the 8:00 to 8:45 p.m. Bible study, you might use one of the Mastering the Basics study guides prepared by Lyman Coleman and Richard Peace. Several options are available including *The Sermon on the Mount, Parables,* and *1 and 2 Timothy.* (You may order the books by calling Serendipity House, Littleton, CO 80160; toll free 1 800 525-9563.) The studies almost lead themselves and give helpful hints on facilitating a healthy group. You may need to do some selective choosing of discussion questions. Of course, you may find other helpful Bible study resources.

A twelve-week model training program including a weekly Bible study, a chapter from *Called to Care,* and an application exercise would look as follows.

Serendipity Bible Study Chapter	*Called to Care* Training Chapter	*Application*
1.	1. The Nurture Group	Our Group Covenant
2.	2. The Support Group	Self-Disclosure

3.	3. The Evangelistic Group	Networks
4.	4. The Mission Group	Our Group's Purpose
5.	5. Acceptance	Sharing Questions
6.	6. Bible Study	Preparation
7.	7. Prayer	Prayer
8.	8. Mission	Our Group's Mission
9.	9. Leadership	Leadership
10.	10. Group Participation	Participation
11.	11. Creativity and Conflict	Conflict Resolution
12.	12. Supervision and Cont. Ed.	Your Small Group Dream

How Will You Help Each Potential Leader?

Carefully read *Called to Care* in its entirety. Lead the first several meetings yourself. Ask a sharing question, lead a Bible study, and lead in sharing and prayer as outlined in chapters 5-8 of *Called to Care*. Then teach one chapter each week from *Called to Care* with its accompanying application exercise. You may want to begin your teaching time with the application exercise.

After you have modeled a few sessions, give each member of the group an opportunity to lead a meeting (except for the *Called to Care* and application exercise portion, which you will always do). Your group members will learn best by doing! Agree who will take which sessions by writing their names by the appropriate weeks in the above schedule.

It will be your challenge to help each member do the best job possible of leading. You want them to do it again and again on their own! Consider the following steps for helping your group members lead a session.

1. Before the group meeting, meet with the person who will be leading. Insist on this one-on-one meeting! It is essential. Go over the person's lesson plan and the chapter you will be teaching from *Called to Care*. Is the leader's aim clear and valid? Are discussion questions open-ended and focused in the direction of the aim? Has the leader done the necessary background research? Are there parts of the study or evening that should be omitted?

Give special attention to the part of the study that will receive focus via the application exercise in *Called to Care*. Put extra effort into that part of the meeting but do not call attention to it. Pray with your potential leader.

2. As the group meeting begins, introduce the student leader. Set an enthusiastic tone for the leader. Assist where you can, but let the person lead. Don't take back the responsibility for leading that you have delegated to the student leader. Be encouraging.

3. At the end of each session take responsibility for leading and teaching the application exercise and chapter from *Called to Care*. Give the group time to complete the application exercise. Then discuss it. Give as much positive feedback as you can to that day's leader! If correction is needed, reserve as much of it as possible for a private meeting.

4. After the group meeting, meet one-on-one with the student leader. Discuss the experience of leading the meeting. Listen actively to his or her feelings. Explore them carefully. Build up positives, work through negatives. A good evaluation will inspire the person to try again. Explore what the leader learned from the experience and would do differently next time. Challenge the person toward becoming a lay pastor-leader of a Care Group.

What Are the Essentials?

During the training experience, you will want to give priority to helping your potential leaders learn three basic leadership skills. These skills, when practiced carefully, will make a major difference in the dynamics of a Care Group. Challenge them with the following:

1. The skill of active listening. Active listening more than anything else will tell your group members that you care about them and what is happening in their lives. Attentive listening will also have tremendous benefits for you. If you want to be liked by your group, listen actively! If you want to become wise, listen carefully to their wisdom! If you want to be effective, listen attentively to their needs! Try to learn everything you can about each of your group members. (For more on active listening, see chapter 5 in *Called to Care*.)

2. The skill of asking questions. Your goal is good dialogue, not a good lecture. Never give information that the student can discover through asking good questions! Good sharing questions help members to feel accepted. Good discussion questions help students discover the truth of a Scripture or topic. Questions need to be open-ended. This means they cannot be answered by a simple yes or no. Questions from the group should usually be redirected back to the group for exploration or response. (For more on the art of asking questions, see chapters 5 and 6 in *Called to Care*.)

3. The skill of dialogue. Preaching and teaching have been the dominant forms of communication in the church. Care Groups will seek to balance these forms of monologue by emphasizing dialogue. Good dialogue begins with good listening. Before responding to a statement, you should often verify through a reflective response what you have understood the speaker to say. In good dialogue, conversation moves back and forth between participants. (Chapter 10 in *Called to Care* has more on the art of dialogue.)

Summary Checklist for Training Leaders
____**Step 1: Choose a training model.**

There are two ways to train leaders. The first is to lead a model training group for thirteen weeks. See Resource 8, Twelve-Week Model Training Group. An alternative is to

have a concentrated experience as outlined in Resource 7,
Leadership Training Seminar.

___Step 2: Choose a time and place for the first meeting.
If you choose the thirteen-week model, announce a time
and place most agreeable to the potential members. Use
chapter 1 in *Called to Care* as your guide for coming to
agreement on your elements of covenant.

___Step 3: Lead the first several sessions.
Lead the first several sessions of the training group. At
the end of each session help the group evaluate both your
leadership and their participation patterns. If you are doing the one-day seminar, seek to do your very best in leading the "fishbowl" experience. It will be evaluated in nu-
merous ways during the day.

___Step 4: Give each member an opportunity to lead.
Assist each member of the group in preparing and leading
one session. Have a one-on-one meeting with each potential leader both before and after this experience.

___Step 5: Teach thirteen aspects of group life.
Take twenty minutes each week (or in a one-day experience according to Resource 7) to highlight the assigned
chapter in *Called to Care* and to lead the discussion aris-
ing from the evaluation exercise. Drive home the main
point of each chapter!

___Step 6: Prepare the potential leaders for their own
groups.
As the training program comes into its final weeks, help
group members decide whether or not they want to pro-
ceed with leading a group. Help them choose an apprentice or partner, and the type of group they might like to

lead. Assist in selecting possible study materials and exploring possible persons to invite. (Questions to help you in this process can be found at the end of chapters 9 to 12 in *Called to Care*.)

____**Step 7: Look forward to supervision and continuing education.**

As you lead the model training sessions, help your potential leaders to look forward positively to the ongoing supervision and continuing education experiences they will be receiving each month after they begin leading a group.

____**Step 8: Evaluate the training experience.**

At the end of the first and last sessions, ask the participants for feedback on the training experience. What was most helpful? What should be repeated? What could be done better next time? Use Resource 9, Training Evaluation Form, after the final session so you can improve your skills next time around.

RESOURCE 7

One Day Leadership Training Seminar

8:30 - 9:00	Registration and Warm-Up
9:00 - 9:20	Sharing the Vision (Prologue Called to Come)
9:20 - 10:00	Types of Groups: (Chapters 1-4)
10:00 - 10:15	Coffee Break
10:15 - 11:00	A Care Group in a Fishbowl (Chapters 5-8)

  • Welcome and sharing question—15 minutes
  • Bible study in dialogue form—20 minutes
  • Personal sharing and prayer—10 minutes

11:00 - 11:20	The Importance of Sharing Questions (Chapter 5)

  • Write and practice sharing questions

11:20 - 11:40	Bible Study in Dialogue Form (Chapter 6)

  • Write an aim and three discussion questions

11:40 - 12:00	Prayer: A Conversation with God (Chapter 7)

  • Model conversational prayer

12:00 -1:00	LUNCH
1:00-1:20	Mission: What will you do? (Chapter 8)

  • Brainstorm mission possibilities

1:20 -2:00	Leadership Issues: (Chapters 9-11)

  • Identify your leadership style
  • Practice active listening and dialogue skills

2:00 - 2:30	Recruiting and Beginning a Group (See chapter 5 from this manual, *Called to Equip*)

  • Prepare an invitee list and initial covenant

2:30 -3:30	Supervision in a Fishbowl (Chapter 12)

  • Discuss possible continuing education themes

3:30 -4:00	Plan Next Steps and Close

  • Evaluate the day
  • Plan for the commissioning service

RESOURCE 8

Thirteen-Week Model Training Group

1. Purpose: • To model a Care Group including its usual components of fellowship, Bible study, sharing, and prayer.
 • To teach the skills needed for leading a group by demonstration and supervised practice.
 • To coach potential group leaders in how to begin and lead a group.

2. Materials: Each participant will need a Bible study guide as decided by the group plus a copy of *Called to Care*. One chapter from each will be studied each week. If you need to abbreviate the experience, combine chapters 1 through 4 into one session. If absolutely necessary, chapters 9 through 11 can also be combined.

3. Schedule: The group will seek to meet for two hours once each week for thirteen weeks. The schedule will look something like the following.

7:30-8:00	Welcome and opening sharing question
8:00-8:45	Bible study using a dialogue form
8:45-9:00	Personal sharing and prayer
9:00-9:20	Study one chapter from *Called to Care*
9:20-9:30	Closing and refreshments

RESOURCE 9

Training Evaluation Form
(To be filled out after training)

Please fill out this form as it applies to your experience in the Care Group leader training program. Thank you for helping us improve it. You need not sign your name.

1. How many sessions have you attended?

2. How would you rate the training program?

____Excellent ____Good ____Fair ____Poor

3. What one thing do you feel has been *most effective* in this training program and should be continued?

4. What one thing do you think has been *least helpful* and could be discontinued?

5. What one thing might be added to make this training program *more effective*?

6. Comments about facilities, materials, instruction, etc., that might be helpful.

_____
Signature optional

4 Commissioning Leaders

Why Have a Commissioning?

A church can scuttle its Care Group ministry by not commissioning its leaders. Without the benefits of commissioning, the ministry will tend to lack focus, identity, and a sense of importance. Four specific values may be noted.

• Commissioning Care Group leaders helps the congregation focus on the gifts God gives his church for caring. It provides an opportunity for celebration of these gifts.

• Commissioning helps the congregation experience ownership of the Care Group ministry. Through a commissioning service, the congregation expresses approval and support for the program and persons in it.

• Commissioning provides an opportunity for the pastor to explain what leaders do and how they relate to the pastoral team. It clarifies the identity and the accountability of Care Group leaders.

• Commissioning helps the Care Group leaders by providing them personal and spiritual support. It gives the congregation an opportunity to pledge prayer and moral support.

What Principles Should Be Followed?

Make commissioning honest. Commission only those qualified. This will require a personal interview with each person who has expressed interest in being a Care Group leader. (See Resource 10, Interview with Potential Care Group Leader for an outline.) A church board member may assist with the interview. Five purposes for the one-on-one interview might be highlighted.

1. To explore the motives for desiring to be a Care Group leader. Primarily whose needs will be met, the leader's or the group's?

2. To discern the qualities the person has and wants to develop. Is this person hospitable, respected, and sensitive?

3. To go over the job description and clarify responsibilities and patterns of accountability. Is he or she willing to commit to supervision?

4. To explain the commissioning service. What promises will be made? Who will do what?

5. To answer any questions the person might have about forming a group, leading it, and maintaining confidentiality in ministry.

Make commissioning special. Commissioning can be a time for the congregation to recommit itself to being a caring church! Prepare in advance through a bulletin announcement, a newsletter article, and possibly a press release. Have a precommissioning breakfast or post-commissioning dinner with those commissioned. Take pictures for keepsake or for a future slide or video show which will depict the Care Group ministry.

Make commissioning beautiful. Prepare for an artistic ceremony. Have someone make an appropriate banner. Plan for special music, flowers, or prayers.

Make commissioning meaningful. Affirm before the entire congregation your pastoral ideals for a team ministry. Allow other Care Group leaders to assist in welcoming new team members. Use commissioning statements that are honest expressions of your feelings, of the new commitments being made, and of the congregation's support.

What Form Will the Service Take?

Following is a commissioning service you might want to choose from or refer to as a frame of reference. It is based on a service prepared by Stephen Ministries, an interdenominational organization dedicated to the training of lay caregivers for the church.[11]

The Introduction

_____*(name or names)*_____, you have been called and equipped to serve as a lay pastor (or Care Group leader) here at the _____ Church. We wish to acknowledge your willingness to serve and want to affirm that we believe God will use you to build his church. This is not a small responsibility to which you are being called. It involves (outline the responsibilities).

We are encouraged by the words of the apostle Paul who said (read 2 Cor. 1:3-4 and/or Col. 3:23-24).

The Call and Commitment

Ask Care Group leaders to make a statement regarding their call and commitment. Or you may want to ask one or two of the following questions:

We know from your private [or public] testimony that you are experiencing Jesus Christ as Lord and Savior of your life. Will you now walk with the members of a Care Group who need the teaching, forgiveness, comfort, and guidance you are receiving?

As the Lord Jesus patiently listens when you turn to him, will you be a regular and patient listener to the members of your group?

As the Spirit of Christ has given you skills and abilities, will you use them to help the members of your Care Group so they will be able to study the Scriptures together, to share with each other, pray for one another, and bring each other to wholeness in Christ?

Are you prepared to assist the pastor as you serve the members of a Care Group in this congregation?

The Congregation's Affirmation

Will you as a congregation affirm these individuals as Care Group leaders [or assistants to the pastor] of _____ _____ Church who are being commissioned to lead some of us in Bible study, sharing, prayer, and mission? Will you open your hearts to the ministry of these persons, to pray for them, and encourage them so they may be effective servants of Christ?

The Charge and Prayer

_____, I commend you to the care and guidance of the Holy Spirit as you care for others. Work hard. Use the gifts you have received and the skills you have learned so you may bless those entrusted to your care.

Father, we ask you to take our sister(s) _____ and our brother(s) _____ into your care. You have blessed them with gifts and talents and are now giving them an opportunity to serve even as they have been served. Help them to be patient in listening, quick to care, and willing to share themselves with those with whom they will be working.

Give to us thankful hearts for their willingness to serve. Keep us all strong in the faith and eager to invite others into the fellowship that you have given to us through Jesus Christ our Lord. Amen.

The Blessing

You may want to choose a blessing from among the following for each of the persons being commissioned.

May the Lord Jesus who has graciously called you to be his disciple, now strengthen you with his Spirit for your ministry in his church and to his world.

May the peace of God free you from the burdens of this life, and enable you to share God's love with the people he is giving into your care.

May God bless you richly, that you may be a blessing to others.

May the Spirit dwell in you richly, filling you with joy and peace and courage for every endeavor that you will face in the Lord's service.

Go in peace. Serve the Lord with gladness.

(Some congregations may choose to give the commissioned a certificate, a handshake, or special reception.)

Summary Checklist for Commissioning Leaders

_____**Step 1: Choose and prepare the person to be commissioned.**

Meet with the person to be commissioned for a personal interview. Use Resource 10, Interview with Potential Care Group Leader. Be convinced that the person has the spiritual qualities needed to minister to the members of a group. Willingness and commitment are not sufficient. Go over the job description. Explore alternatives with those who do not have the needed qualifications.

_____**Step 2: Invite the church board to affirm the commissioning.**

Bring a recommendation to your church governing body encouraging the commissioning of persons for leading a Care Group. Make proper introductions. Present the persons' qualifications for ministry, record of training, and willingness to be in ongoing supervision and continuing education. A brief testimony and time of sharing is in order.

____**Step 3: Announce the commissioning service.**
Announce the commissioning service in the bulletin and possibly even in a press release to your denominational or community newspaper. A brief outline of duties and responsibilities as suggested in Resource 11 might be included in a bulletin announcement.

____**Step 4: Prepare for the service.**
Agree with the persons to be commissioned on the form and questions of commitment to be used. Contact other persons who might be involved. Seek to involve other Care Group leaders. Plan for special music and decor. Reflect on an appropriate pattern of affirmation.

____ **Step 5: Lead the commissioning experience.**
Plan and lead a service that is right for the persons and occasion.

RESOURCE 10

Interview with Potential Care Group Leader

Name _____

Background and Qualifications

1. Could you share a brief faith pilgrimage story? How would you describe your relationship with Jesus Christ? What has been your experience with the church?
2. On a scale of one to ten, how convinced are you about the Care Group ministry of our church?
3. What has been your experience and struggle in relationship to being:
   > a. Hospitable. How do you show warmth and friendliness? When and in what ways do you feel uncomfortable when in a group?
   > b. Respected. How do you assess the respect and trust people have for you in your family and community?
   > c. Sensitive. How sensitive are you to other people's needs? Has God given you the ability to sense their concerns?
   > d. Self-control. What habits are you seeking to overcome?
   > e. Motivated. How enthused are you about your faith, your church, and your pastor? How is your personal devotional life going?
   > f. Grounded. How well do you know the Scriptures? How well do you know and how strongly do you affirm the history, purposes, and principles of our congregation?

Job Description and Accountability

1. Do you have any questions about the job description? Read it together.
2. How do you feel about being part of a monthly supervisory and continuing education group? Clarify that it is required.
3. What kind of a group would you like to lead? Who might the members be? Who might serve as your apprentice? What study resources might be used?

RESOURCE 11

Sample Bulletin Announcement and Press Release

Bulletin Announcement

_____(names)_____ will be commissioned on ____(date)_____ to assist in the pastoral ministry of this church as Care Group leaders. They have agreed to initially volunteer their time for the next _____(period of time)_____. Each will:

- Serve as a pastor-facilitator to one of the congregation's Care Groups.
- Attend regular supervision meetings on a monthly basis.
- Maintain confidentiality concerning nonpublic information shared with them.

Let us be thankful for their willingness and prepare ourselves for the commissioning experience.

Press Release

_____(number)_____ additional Care Group Leaders will be commissioned at _____ Church this Sunday, ____(date)____ at ____ (time) ____ to assist in the pastoral ministry of the congregation. Those being commissioned include _____, _____, and _____. They have finished the congregation's Care Group training program.

Care Group leaders under the supervision of _____ _____, pastor of the church, each provide pastoral care for up to twelve members of the congregation together with their families.

Care Groups meet weekly in homes for fellowship, Bible study, personal sharing, and prayer. Group members agree to give priority to the meeting, to keep what is shared in the group confidential, and to be available to each other in time of need.

5 Beginning the Groups

Who Needs a Group?

Everyone needs some kind of a group. Hermits are considered strange because for various reasons they deny their need for others. Sociologists tell us that most people engage in a persistent search for a group that will provide them with a sense of belonging.

Groups help us make decisions and follow through on them. Care Groups are, in effect, Christian peer groups that can have a powerful effect on our lives. Baptism and church membership have to do with joining a Christian peer group. Evangelism has to do with inviting someone to become part of a peer group where they can meet Christ and like-minded persons.

A group begins when someone brings together several —perhaps three to twelve persons—who have a common interest or need. The leader then helps potential members agree on a common purpose and format. Small groups happen all the time. Some are informal groupings while others are more carefully planned. Churches that are intentional about small groups and offer proper supervision are less likely to have cliques than those who do not.

A congregation is a collection of groups. A healthy congregation has seven to ten groups per hundred attenders. Generally, the more face-to-face groups in a congregation, the faster it grows.

New people need new groups. It is easier for new people to establish deep relationships with one another when networks of relationships are still comparatively new and flexible. Kennon L. Callahan in *Twelve Keys to an Effective Church* says, "Those churches that quit starting new groups are churches that have decided to die. Those churches that thoughtfully and intentionally start a range of new groups are those churches that have decided to grow."[12]

We can learn from the strategy of InterVarsity's work on college campuses. InterVarsity leaders carefully study their campus and identify the various groupings. These might include students in dorms, ethnic groups, and academic interest groups. They pray for an open door to each group. Their long-range aspiration is that, in time, "every campus grouping will have a small group of Christians in it, actively working to share the gospel with every person."[13] What are the groupings in your church and community?

Most every congregation has age groups—children, youth, young adults, seniors. It seems each age group in the church needs at least one group. Newcomers of that age group will often find comradeship in the group.

Within every congregation there are also a variety of cultures. There is the youth culture. There may also be persons representing a 1960s mentality or the 1930s depression years. Congregations may have groups of people who were born and raised in another state or part of the world. People of each culture and ethnic group have a need to belong. Jesus commissioned us to "make disciples of all peoples!"

Also within each congregation and community are people with special needs. There are single parents, persons in grief, those struggling with bankruptcy, divorce, drugs, or a particular illness. Resource 12, Care Group Invitee Worksheet, will help you develop a grid of the members in your church community and to see the possible need for groups.

Finally, people gather around common interests. People look for others whose interests resemble their own. It may be an interest in Bible study, sharing, and prayer. Or an interest in evangelism, ecological farming, a community mission project, or beginning a mediation program. A Care Group leader who shares a common interest with others may be effective in helping them to begin a group. Take time to work on Resource 12 or have your church secretary do it. Don't only exegete Scripture. Exegete your congregation and community!

How Will Potential Group Members Be Invited?

People will be most likely to respond to an invitation from a fellow member of their group or culture. The key to establishing a Care Group in every grouping of the church and community is to recruit and train a leader from that grouping and have that person invite peers. If more groups are needed in that grouping, that initial leader can aid in recruiting and training apprentices.

Groups need to be voluntary. Never force people into groups. People with common needs and interests must be helped to find each other!

Most groups in the church will likely arise out of a need for Bible study, sharing, and prayer leading to deeper spiritual life. But also provide your group leaders with the research on groupings from Resource 12. Help them know their own selves. What are their needs? What grouping and culture do they represent? Where do they belong?

Assist them in coming to a decision by filling out Resource 13, Pre-Group Invitation Planning Sheet—which will help them clarify their own need, make a possible invitee list of other persons who have that need, and write a clear purpose statement for the group. Ask each potential Care Group leader to check their Pre-Group Invitation Planning Sheet with you before they begin inviting persons for their potential group.

After a discussion with potential Care Group leaders, encourage them to extend an invitation to invitees for an initial exploration meeting. The invitation may be in the form of a personal conversation, a phone call, or a letter followed by a phone call. Resource 14, A Sample Letter of Invitation, provides a possible format for a letter.

A general rule is that Care Group leaders will need to invite a third more persons to the exploratory meeting than they hope will finally be in the group. In other words, if they want six in the group, they should invite eight to the initial meeting.

Not everyone will respond positively. Don't take no as a permanent answer. As time goes by, find ways to keep talking with each person in the church (and even in the community) until each has found a group that suits his or her need!

An alternative to Care Group leaders choosing potential members is to allow a group of individuals, or even the whole congregation, to indicate whom they would like to have lead them and what they would like to have as the focal purpose for their group(s). Resource 15, Which Care Group for You? is a way of helping individuals choose a group. If you follow this pattern, or use this resource on Sunday morning, you as pastor may want to preach a sermon on the value of having groups. After the forms are turned in, you or the Care Group coordinator will need to tabulate them and help bring interested persons together according to preferences.

Generally the majority of a group should be homogeneous or like-minded persons. But several heterogeneous, non-like-minded persons from a different background, might be beneficial. A variety of age, gender, and background can add interest to group life. The non-like persons will often be the ones to interject the interesting questions and experiences that will keep the group lively and relevant. (Chapters 2 through 5 of *Called to Care* offer additional help for the forming of nurture, support, evangelistic, and mission Care Groups.)

If all of this sounds too complicated, remember a group can be formed any time two or three people agree on a common covenant consistent with your vision and/or guidelines for Care Groups. You may want to begin with just one group the first year. If the initial members in that Care Group experience the deep care of their leader and engage in honest dialogue with each other, they will capture the vision and tell others of the benefits they are finding in the group.

What Happens at the First Meeting?

It is almost impossible to overestimate the importance of a group's first meeting. The impressions created usually influence the group's progress for weeks to come.

You need to encourage your Care Group leader to be a leader, but not an autocrat with an air of superiority. An unpretentious, honest spirit that has in mind the best interests of each group member goes a long way. A group leader will be on "probation" until the group members are convinced he or she is there for their good.

At the first meeting, members need to get acquainted with each other. As each person arrives, make sure they know everyone else present. Help the members get to know each other by having each share something about themselves. Start with names, history-giving, hometown, and occupations. Unusual and unimportant questions like, "What did you have for breakfast?" help everyone stay relaxed.

The following is suggested as a time flow for the first evening meeting.

7:30 Welcome, refreshments and get acquainted question
8:00 Bible study (perhaps just study one verse such as
     1 John 4:12)

8:15 Clarify your covenant. Five aspects are generally clarified:

- Agreement on purpose—Why do you want to meet?
- Agreement on format—What will a usual meeting include?
- Agreement on leadership—Who is to lead and how?
- Agreement on logistics—Where, when and how long will the meetings be?
- Agreement on ground rules—Questions about attendance, confidentiality, availability, and childcare need to be addressed.

Summary Checklist for Beginning Care Groups

____ **Step 1: Assess the need and readiness**.

Begin by assessing your own need and readiness. Perhaps from September to November you personally want to begin one group without a grand plan. During the fall, allow the members to read your copy of *Called to Care*.

If you are beyond this stage, do an assessment of how many potential Care Group leaders you have and how many you will need. How many people have expressed interest in being part of a group? How many groupings are there in the church and community into which you would like to plant a Care Group? (See Resource 12, Care Group Invitee Worksheet.) Report your findings and your decisions or recommendations to your church board or council.

____ **Step 2: Help Care Group leaders recruit**.

Help each Care Group leader fill out Resource 13, Pre-Group Invitation Work Sheet. This will give you an opportunity to assist the leader in developing an invitee list and a focus for the potential group. Assist the leader in deciding on a strategy for inviting. Share Resource 14, A Sample Letter of Invitation. Explore with the leader whether or not an open invitation to the exploration meeting should be extended to the congregation.

_____ **Step 3: Preach a supportive sermon**.
In September when groups usually form or reform, preach a sermon that restates the vision you have for the church and indicates how Care Groups will help make it a reality. Write an article for your newsletter, make presentations at Sunday school and Sunday evening meetings, and in other ways support formation of Care Groups.

_____**Step 4: Help leaders plan and evaluate their first meeting**.
Meet with each potential leader. Go over the plans for the first meeting. Discuss the leader's attitude toward the group and experience. Explore purpose, format, and logistics for the first meeting. Meet again for a supportive time of evaluation and planning after the first meeting has taken place. Pray for and with each leader. Share the schedule and expectations for the peer supervision and continuing education meetings.

RESOURCE 12

Care Group Invitee Worksheet
(To be completed by church secretary)

Go through the congregation's address or telephone directory and categorize the people by name into the following groupings. You will need to use extra sheets of paper. Explore the possibility of planting a Care Group into each of the groupings. Seek to develop groupings of more than five but less than twenty.

A. Age for Sunday School Groupings (List all persons)

0 - 9	40 - 49
10 - 19	50 - 59
20 - 29	60 - 69
30 - 39	70 -

B. Place of Origin and Cultural Groupings

Group the people of the congregation by place of origin and other types of cultural background. Which people have not grown up in the community or which have grown up in other churches or situations and have a special need to belong? Use the categories for analysis only. Don't "label" people in your relationships.

Asian	Depression survivors	Other
African-American	Baby Boomers	Other
Hispanic	Social activists	
Other	Self-actualizers	

C. Unchurched Groupings

Inactive members

Husbands of wives who attend

Extended family

New residents

D. Special Needs/Situations

Newly married
Parenting Preschoolers
Parenting teenagers
Single parents
Marriage enrichment
Midlife crises
Divorce recovery

RESOURCE 13

Pre-Group Invitation Planning Sheet
(For discussion by potential leader and pastor)

Potential group leader _____ Phone _____

My need for a group: _____

Potential group members _____ _____

                                        _____ _____

                                        _____ _____

                                        _____ _____

                                        _____ _____

                                        _____ _____

Results hoped for: _____

                           _____

                           _____

Type of group:

       _____Nurture group (Bible study, sharing, prayer)

       _____Support group (parenting, divorce recovery, etc.)

       _____Evangelistic group (half of group nonchurched)

       _____Mission group (special project on ministry)

Logistics:

    Date/time: _____

    Place: _____

    Food: _____

    Children: _____

    Other: _____

Game plan for first meeting:

RESOURCE 14

A Sample Letter of Invitation and Bulletin Announcement

Dear _____ _____

_____ _____

_____ _____

_____ _____

_____ and I would like to invite you
to our house on _____
at _____ for an evening of discussion and brainstorming
about Care Groups. At _____
Church, we have been talking about the need for Care Groups.
We would like to explore possibilities with you.

I would personally like a Care Group that would meet every other
Sunday night. We might meet in each other's homes on a rota-
tion basis.

What would be our focus? We might study the Sermon on the
Mount, the Parables, or 1 and 2 Timothy. There are excellent materials available from Serendipity House that could help us have
good dialogue. The evening might include relaxed fellowship, Bible study, sharing, and prayer, but I am open to your thoughts
and needs.

I am sending this to the eight of you. Can you think of someone
else who might be interested?

I will call you in a few days to confirm whether or not you can
come. Let me assure you there will be no obligation after this first
evening to be part of a group. We simply want to explore the
possibilities and go from there.

Talk to you soon,

Bulletin Announcement

Care Groups are becoming the key pastoral structure of our church. On a regular basis, under the guidance of a lay leader, they provide attenders with opportunities for Christian fellowship, Bible study, personal sharing, and prayer. If you would like to explore being part of one of these groups, you are invited to one of the following homes:

Host/Leader	Location	Phone	Day	Time	Code
Adrian/Becker	1018 N 10th Street,	427-2232	Su	7:00 pm	C
Hoffman/Harder	704 3rd Avenue,	427-5894	W	9:00 am	W

Code
C = Couples; W = Women only; M = Men only; CS = Couples and singles; SP = Special

Your name _____

Which Care Group for You?
(For use by the entire congregation)

All of us have a need to belong. Some of us belong to family, work, or peer groups. At _____ Church we want to have enough options that everyone can also belong to a Care Group. We call them Care Groups because they are where we find a caring quality of fellowship, study, sharing, and prayer.

We will not force anyone into a group. We want you to choose a group or to be chosen by someone already in a group. Can you help us? What kind of a group would interest you? Four types are described. Which would meet your need? Check your first and second choice. We will do our best to get you an invitation!

Nurture Groups

Nurture groups are primarily for Christians who want to grow. Nurture groups will generally meet weekly in homes. They will include light refreshments, fellowship, study-dialogue, sharing, and prayer. Some will seek to have a special project. We will practice an "empty chair" which will cause us to ask, "Who else might benefit from this group?" Following are Bible study options (available from Faith and Life Press, 800 743-2484 and Serendipity House, 800 525-9563). If you want to be in a nurture group, check your first, second, and third preference.

Faith and Life Bible Series
____Genesis 1 - 11
____Isaiah
____Colossians
____1 Peter
____Revelation
____Other

Serendipity Materials
____Sermon on the Mount
____Parables
____Romans
____1 Corinthians
____1 and 2 Timothy
____Other

Support Groups

Support groups are for persons both in church and community who are facing a special challenge or difficulty. Most groups will meet for seven sessions. Group meetings will include refreshments and fellowship, study of a Bible passage related to the challenge or difficulty, and sharing/prayer. Study materials are available in the following areas from Serendipity House.

Special Needs
____Dealing with Grief and Loss
____Midlife: The Crises that Brings Renewal
____Compassion Fatigue: Worn Out from Caring
____Unemployed/Unfulfilled: The Most Difficult Job
____Single Again: Life After Divorce

Marriage Enrichment
____Newly Married: How to Have a Great First Year
____The Golden Years: Myths and Realities of Aging
____Infertility: Coping with the Pain of Childlessness
____Remaining Married: Learning to Deal with Issues
____Engaged: Are You Fit to be Tied?

Parenting
____Parenting Adolescents: Easing the Way
____Blended Families: Yours, Mine, Ours
____Single Parenting: Flying Solo
____Learning Disabilities: Parenting the Misunderstood
____Parenting Preschoolers

Recovery
____12 Steps: The Path to Wholeness
____Addictive Lifestyles
____Adult Children of Alcoholics
____Codependency: Learning to Say "Enough"
____Eating Disorders: When Food Is the Enemy

Evangelistic Groups

Evangelistic groups seek to bring non-Christians into meaningful relationship with Jesus Christ. To be part of an evangelistic group, you need to bring along a non-Christian friend or relative. The meetings will include refreshments and fellowship, a study of Jesus, and comfortable dialogue about him. Evangelism groups meet for seven sessions. Options for study might involve:

____ *Who is this Jesus?* Michael Green.
____ *Gospel of Man?* Serendipity House.

Mission Groups

Mission groups begin when someone sounds a call and invites those interested to form a group that will seek to bring resources or solution to a need. Mission groups might address a need in either church or community—relating to an ethnic group, a socio-economic concern, or some special emotional or spiritual need. What mission is calling you? _____

6 Supervising Leaders

Supervision is the Key to Quality Christian Care in Groups!

Supervision is a supportive relationship between two or more persons to improve the quality of ministry being offered. Because supervision is key, it is a requirement in the Care Group ministry. A Care Group whose leader or facilitator is not in supervision will not be listed as a group that is being sponsored by the church. A schedule for supervision and continuing education sessions should be developed and announced on commissioning Sunday. (See Resource 21, Schedule for Supervisory/Continuing Education Meetings.)

The following guidelines are based on those developed over many years and tested in thousands of settings by Stephen Ministries. They are commended to you with confidence.[14]

Why Have Supervision?

There are three reasons supervision is an important requirement.

1. Supervision is for the sake of the Care Group members.

Supervision enables leaders to offer the best possible leadership and the best possible care to the Care Group members. Leaders know they can minister more effectively when they have been helped to reflect on their ministry, to solve problems, and to set new goals.

2. Supervision is for the sake of the Care Group leaders. Under your guidance and through mutual collaboration, Care Group leaders are helped to do their best. Leaders attend supervision because they care about themselves and about the ministry of fellow group leaders. Leaders not only receive supervision, they also participate in giving it to each other.

3. Supervision is for the sake of you, the pastor. Supervision is a way for you, the pastor or Care Group coordinator, to care for your group leaders. Supervision is not to be confused with dictatorial shepherding in which an authority places requirements on an individual, then demands strict submission. Supervision is where you listen to and care for your team. You give them the opportunity to learn more skills. In problem solving, you help Care Group leaders explore options, then let them make the final decisions. As you grow close, you will experience the joys that come from partnership in the gospel.

Who Does the Supervision?

You are responsible as pastor to convene and facilitate the monthly meetings of the Care Group leaders. The group leaders, however, supervise each other—through what might be called "collaborative peer supervision." Your primary task is not to evaluate the performance of your leaders or teach them a new skill. It is to listen and to lead a dialogue so leaders will experience self-improvement.

As pastor, it is one of your responsibilities to print and keep your leaders supplied with the resource and check-in sheets that help to guide the process.

The organizational structure for a congregation with eight

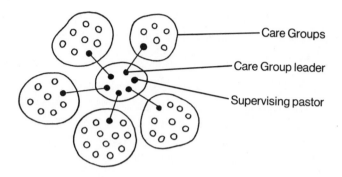

Care Groups

Care Group leader

Supervising pastor

or less groups might look something like the following.

If there are more than eight Care Groups in your church, you will need to divide the leaders into smaller groups of five to eight for supervision. You will determine how the leaders are grouped. Take age, gender, experience, and group-dynamic skills into consideration in forming these smaller supervisory groups.

Appoint one person from each smaller supervisory group to be a facilitator. Carefully go over the materials in this chapter with facilators. Meet with them after each meeting to see how things went. Help them do a good job of facilitating.

The organizational structure for a congregation with more than eight groups might look more like this.

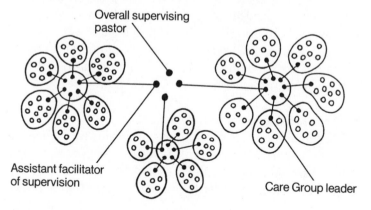

Overall supervising pastor

Assistant facilitator of supervision

Care Group leader

What Happens in Supervision?

A suggested schedule for a two-hour supervision/continuing education meeting is as follows:

Opening	(all group leaders together)	5 minutes
Peer supervision	(leaders in groups of 5 to 8)	55 minutes
Break	(all group leaders together)	15 minutes
Continuing education	(all group leaders together)	40 minutes
Closing	(all group leaders together)	5 minutes

Note the brevity of the opening, the break, and the closing. These time limits should be carefully followed so the fifty-five minutes for peer supervision and the forty minutes for continuing education can be protected. When there is a conflict and something needs to be cut, priority should be given to supervision. Meetings should start and end on time.

There are four steps to the fifty-five minutes of supervision time.

1. An overall view One minute
Individually greet and welcome your Care Group leaders. As they arrive, ask them to lend to you their Weekly Care Group Record Sheet, Resource 16. This sheet will give you an overall view of what is happening in each group. Take a quick look at it to review: Who is in the group? How often has it been meeting? And how has the leader evaluated the group experiences? After the Care Group leader has given a check-in report (see next item) return the Weekly Care Group Record Sheet.

2. Check-in Statements Ten minutes
The fifty-five minute supervision time begins with a one- or two-minute check-in statement from each Care Group leader. This is based on the Monthly Leader's Check-in Sheet, Resource 17. Ask each leader to prepare this check-in sheet in

advance and bring it to the meeting. The following instructions appear on the back of that resource sheet.

A check-in statement should be—

a. Brief. It should give the basic facts about the group. What is it studying? What else is going on in the group? The report should not be more than two minutes in length.

b. Honest. The report needs to be honest about what is and what is not happening in the group and ministry. If leaders are feeling uncomfortable, afraid, or concerned about some aspect of their leadership or ministry, that is exactly what the report should be about! Encourage vulnerability!

c. Confidential. A check-in report should never mention names. If someone guesses who a "problem person" is, encourage confidentiality. Seek to be professional by focusing on relationships, not persons involved.

d. Thoughtful. A check-in report should be thought through and prepared before the group leader comes to the meeting. Thought should be given to how the peers in the supervision group might help.

A simple check-in statement might run something like this:

"My Care Group has met regularly during the past month. We are halfway through the gospel of Mark. There are several hurting people in the group who need a listening ear. They are receiving good support from each other and from me. We spend up to half our time in sharing. One person in my group talks too much. She seems to take responsibility for fixing every problem. I am getting quite upset and could use some help on knowing how to relate to this person."

Another leader might check in with this statement:

"My Care Group is going well with one exception. We are experiencing good insights into the challenges of Jesus from our study of the Sermon on the Mount. The group seems to need and appreciate the background I bring to the studies. One problem I am having is that my apprentice has become deeply involved in his university studies and has stopped coming. This peer group could help me explore what I might do."

After each check-in statement, you will want to make a brief response. Give lots of affirmation! Affirm what can be affirmed. If you identify a problem that the two of you might profitably discuss, mention it and after the meeting set up a time to get together. Do not stop to discuss each check-in statement. After all have shared, choose the statement you think most needs attention and spend ten minutes seeking to solve the problem presented. See the next item.

3. Problem Solving Ten minutes

Choose one check-in statement for problem solving. Ask the Care Group leader to describe the problem in greater depth. Ask what he or she has done this far to solve the situation. Do not mention names.

After describing the problem and his or her initial attempts at solution, have the presenter remain silent while you ask the other Care Group leaders to brainstorm what they might do in the situation. Then bring the presenter back into the discussion by asking, "What do you think your next steps might be?" Seek to agree on the best course of action but leave the final decision up to the individual group leader. Stop to pray for the leader.

4. In-depth evaluation of ministry Thirty minutes

After "putting out a fire" as you did above, concentrate on

building the ministry of one group leader. Set up a schedule whereby each Care Group Leader in turn will have the opportunity to present his or her leadership and ministry situation in depth. If possible this should happen semi-annually (see Resource 21).

If another group leader has a major emergency, his or her ministry should be given priority to the one scheduled. An example of an emergency would be if—due to friction, disagreements, or an upsetting event—the future of the group or the future of the group's leadership was in question.

In advance ask the scheduled Care Group leader to fill out the Semi-Annual Ministry Assessment Form, Resource 18, as an aid to sharing his or her leadership and ministry situation. This sharing may take five to eight minutes. The person reporting should honor the priorities of concentration given below.

Priorities of Concentration

a. **Most of the reporting time** concentrate on the group dynamics or what Stephen Ministries calls the *caring relationship*. This is the relationship between the Care Group leader and the group members.

b. **Some of the reporting time** concentrate on the situation and needs of the *leader*—his or her feelings, skill development, spiritual growth, or style.

c. **Occasionally**, concentrate on the situation and needs of the *group* or *group members*.

When a leader has finished the report, begin the evaluation with affirmation. Point out specific things the Care Group leader is doing well. Affirmation builds trust. It allows group leaders to admit weaknesses, which leads to receiving constructive feedback. If the reporting leader seeks to look good, the group will not have much to work with and the help received will be limited. Encourage vulnerable reporting that tells it like it is!

After initial affirmations, ask the presenting leader to nomi-nate a set of focus questions which best apply to the situation (see Resource 19, Focus Questions). Notice the focus ques-tions are arranged in four different sets.

Set A: The group dynamics and the leader's relationship to the group.

Set B: The spiritual nature or concerns related to the caring relationship.

Set C: The group leader's feelings about self, skills, or role.

Set D: The problems or situations of the group members.

Together with your group leaders, choose one or two ques-tions from the set. Use them to explore the Care Group leader's relationships and process. The questions enable the group to examine in depth one aspect of the leader's relationship or ministry. If the group tries without focus to discuss all aspects of the relationship or ministry, it will end up with a shallow, general discussion that leads to little or no learning.

The focus questions are the primary tool for examining the caring relationship between the group leader and group mem-bers. They will help the group get below surface problems to root causes. The questions are open-ended and process-oriented. They will help the presenting leader explore feelings, thoughts, and processes. They will help a leader find the most effective way to give care and leadership to a group.

With experience, the group may want to explore other ways of evaluating and improving ministry, such as:

a. Role-play a situation experienced. Role-plays enable group members to see problem relationships or situa-tions more vividly.

b. Choose a metaphor to describe a situation. For example, "If you were a thermometer, where would your mercury be right now?" or "In what season of the year would you say your relationship is with the group?"

c. A presenting leader may bring for examination a verbatim, without names, of a conversation or group dialogue.

5. Conclusion   Five minutes

Conclude the fifty-five minute time of supervision by asking the presenter to summarize and evaluate what he or she has heard from the group. What has been most helpful? Take a minute to explore how the group could have been more helpful. How can the supervision experience be improved?

End with additional words of affirmation and encouragement. Speak a word of blessing and have a time of prayer with the presenting group leader. Mention who will be presenting at next month's meeting. Clarify date and time. Take a break and come back for forty minutes of continuing education.

What Happens in Continuing Education?

Continuing education topics will focus on concerns and issues which Care Group leaders face in their ministry. Resource 20, Possible Themes for Continuing Education, lists fifteen possible continuing education topics. Ask your leaders to add to the list. Announce additions to leaders, then ask them to prioritize the topics. Help your group leaders deal with the topics one at a time in order of priority. Those who have taken a Stephen Ministries training course will have many resources to draw from. You may need to gather resources from libraries and various other sources.

In continuing education, spend half of the time presenting the topic and the other half in discussing it. The forty minutes designated will go quickly. On occasion you may want to agree on an extension of time. Seek to involve the group through experience-centered learning. Use role-plays or have members share encounters they have had with the issue. How have participants been ministered to or ministered in similar situations? Occasionally bring in outside speakers or films to address a need. When appropriate, open the continuing education experience to the entire church or community.

How Often Should Care Group Leaders Meet?

When group leaders care about each other and their ministries, they want to meet often. It is recommended that group leaders gather for supervision and continuing education once a month except in summer.

But you may want to meet twice a month! Once a month is minimum. If group leaders meet only once per month and someone misses a meeting, two months is a long time between meetings. A lot can happen in a group in that period of time. If a group of seven or eight meets twice a month, each leader's ministry comes up for assessment twice a year instead of only once. To reflect on a leader's ministry once in fall and once in spring helps group leaders to see and affirm progress and direction. For this reason Resource 18 has been titled *semiannual* Ministry Assessment Form.

No supervision at all will kill a Care Group ministry. Without supervision meetings, leaders will not improve skills. They will not enjoy the affirmation and growth that comes from helping each other. They will inevitably lose courage. Make supervision meetings a priority!

What Is the Pastor's Role in Supervision?

You have eight responsibilities in relationship to supervision and continuing education.

1. Convene the group. Set regular times for supervision meetings. Have leaders write meetings into their calendars at the beginning of the year. Choose a place that is private and conducive to good discussion. Set the chairs in a comfortable circle. If you have multiple supervision groups, arrange places for each.

2. Provide resource and check-in sheets. During the training and also for the supervision sessions, various resources and check-in sheets will be needed. Print Resource sheets 16-22 as required and keep your group leaders supplied.

3. Arrange schedules. Schedules should be arranged so all leaders will know when they will have an in-depth evaluation of their ministry. Also arrange the schedules for continuing education. Resource persons need to be contacted well in advance. Resource 21, Schedule for Supervision/Continuing Education Meetings, will help you do the calendar work.

4. Facilitate effective group interaction. Do some fellowship or community-building exercises at the first meeting or two so group members get to know each other's history and values. Model affirmation, actively listen, encourage participation, and reflectively draw out comments, thoughts, and ideas. Don't allow anyone to dominate the group, to criticize, or to condemn another.

5. Promote confidentiality. Concentrate on the ministry that is or is not happening, not on persons in the groups. Model confidentiality by not using names. Remind group members of the need for confidentiality.

6. Keep the group Christ-centered. Help the group recall how Jesus cared for people. Christ-centered caring is unconditional. It flows out of Christ's deep care for us. It focuses on the needs of the other person. When a conversation becomes self-centered, you may need to ask, "Whose needs are being met?" Christian caregivers focus on caring and leave the curing to God's grace.

7. Facilitate periodic evaluation of your supervision sessions. Regular assessment and evaluation of supervision meetings will result in high-quality sessions. Take a minute or two at the end of each supervision session to explore what was helpful and what might be improved. Once or twice a year, use a form to let participants assist in evaluating the supervision experience. Tabulate the results and save ten minutes of time at the next meeting for discussion. (See Resource 22, Evaluation of Supervisory Sessions, for an assessment form.)

8. Assist in closure. When a group of Care Group leaders has shared deeply of themselves and their work, there will be "grieving in the leaving." If a Care Group leader needs to leave an assignment because of a move or some other reason, assist the group in saying farewell. As the year comes to a close, help the members express their feelings, evaluate their performance, reflect on shared experiences, and look to the future. When a previous chapter has been closed honestly and with appreciation, workers will be more ready to start a new one. In May or June, decide on a date for your first meeting of the fall. Plan a social for the summer months.

Summary Checklist for Supervision

_____ **Step 1: Be convinced of the importance of supervision and continuing education.**

Read this chapter carefully. It is the key to offering good pastoral care through a team of lay caregivers.

_____ **Step 2: Convene the Care Group leaders monthly.**

Set a time and place for the monthly meetings. Have each Care Group leader put the dates on his or her calendar. Stress the importance of giving the meetings top priority. Help the leaders decide if they want to meet one or two times per month. Challenge them to see themselves as part of the ministry staff or team.

_____ **Step 3: Divide the Care Group leaders into groups of five to eight.**

If your church has more than eight Care Groups, divide the Care Group leaders into groups of five to eight. You decide how the groups are formed and who should be the facilitator of each group. You probably should not plan for more than eight groups the first year.

____ Step 4: Facilitate the supervisory meetings.

Provide resource sheets and lead the group leaders in a creative dialogue that will help them to help each other. The challenge is to keep the schedule and to ask helpful questions. The four sets of focus questions are prepared to help you. Resources 16–21 should offer the specific help that you need.

____ Step 5: Evaluate the supervisory sessions.

At the end of each supervisory session, help the group to reflect for a minute or two on what was helpful in that month's session and what can be done to make the sessions more helpful. Once or twice a year take a longer period of time to evaluate the sessions using Resource 22, Evaluation of Supervisory Sessions.

____ Step 6: Establish topics and schedules for continuing education.

Help the group leaders to brainstorm and prioritize topics for continuing education. Resources 20 and 21 will help you. Take the lead in arranging and teaching the continuing education topics. It is your opportunity to multiply your ministry to the glory of God!

RESOURCE 16

Weekly Care Group Record Sheet
(For Care Group leaders)

Update this Care Group record sheet after each meeting. Hand it
to your pastor or supervisory group leader as you enter your
monthly meeting. He or she will look it over briefly and hand it
back to you after you make your check-in report.

Regular members		Irregular members
_____	_____	_____
_____	_____	_____
_____	_____	_____
_____	_____	_____
_____	_____	_____

Dates of Mtgs	Atten- dance	No of Guests	Evaluate your experiences 1 = poor; 5 = excellent				Comments
			Fellow- ship	Study	Prayer	Mission	

RESOURCE 17

Monthly Leader's Check-in Sheet
(For Care Group leaders to use in making reports)

Before coming to the monthly supervision meeting, write one- or two-sentence answers to each of the following questions. At the beginning of the meeting, you will have one, or at most two, minutes to share your answers.

1. What is the nature of your group and what is it doing?

2. What do group members need and what are they getting from the group experience?

3. What are your goals for ministry with the group?

4. What is going well in your Care Group and what is not?

5. How can this peer supervisory group help you be a better leader-minister to your group?

(See next page for instructions on how to give a check-in report.)

Giving a Check-in Report

Put careful thought into your check-in report. It is an opportunity to analyze what is happening in your ministry and in your group. The information you put on your check-in report should be:

a. Brief. Give the basic facts about your group and ministry. What are you studying? What else is going on in the group? The report should not be more than two minutes long.

b. Honest. The report needs to be honest about what is happening in the group and in your ministry. If you are feeling uncomfortable, afraid, or concerned about some aspect of your leadership or ministry, that is exactly what the report should be about! Dare to be vulnerable!

c. Confidential. Your check-in report should never mention names. If someone guesses who a "problem person" is in your group, discourage name sharing.

d. Thoughtful. A check-in report should be thought through and prepared before you come to the meeting. Ponder how peers in your supervision group might help you.

A simple check-in statement might run something like this:
"My Care Group has met regularly during the past month. We are halfway through the Gospel of Mark. There are several hurting people in the group who need a listening ear. They are receiving good support from each other and from me. We spend up to half of our time in sharing. One member in my group talks too much. She seems to take responsibility for fixing every problem. I am getting upset and could use some help knowing how to relate to this person."

In your report, seek to honor the priorities of concentration:

• Most of the reporting time concentrate on the *group dynamics* and relationship between you and the group members.

• Some of the reporting time, concentrate on *your own situation and needs*—your feelings, skill development, personal growth, and personal style.

• Occasionally, concentrate on the situation and needs of the *group members*.

Semiannual Ministry Assessment Form
(For Care Group leaders to use in making semiannual in-depth reports)

The purpose of this assessment is to help you reflect on the ministry you are offering to your Care Group and its members. It will assist you in providing pertinent information about your caring relationship to other Care Group leaders in your supervision group so they can help you in your assessment. It aims to help you do an even better job of leading and caring!

This form can be used as an outline for your presentation to the group. Be as complete as possible in your assessment. Use sound judgment as to what you include in your report so confidentiality is protected. Concentrate most on the caring relationship between you and your group. Secondarily give some time to yourself, your feelings, and skills. Try to avoid talking about the situations and problems of your group members. Never mention the names of persons involved unless it is public knowledge and helpful to improving your work.

1. Approximate number of weeks or months that the group has been together. _____
2. In one paragraph describe the needs which brought you and the group together.
   a. Original needs: Are these needs still pressing?
   b. Current goals: Are they clear?
3. Who else is ministering to the members of your group?

   ___ Pastor   ___ Medical personnel
   ___ Public teachers   ___ Sunday school teacher
   ___ Social workers   ___ Other churches
   ___ Other _____   ___ Other_____
   ___ Other _____
4. In one paragraph, summarize how you have been ministering to the persons in this group.

5. Assessment of the caring relationship:
   a. How do you feel about your relationship with the group members?
   b. What has been the nature of the group's response to your ministry?
   c. What has been going well in your relationship?
   d. What has been challenging, frustrating, or problematic?
   e. What do you see as the future direction of your ministry in regard to this group?
6. With what question, concern, issue, or need do you want help at this time?
7. What set of focus questions do you think the supervision group might use to best discuss your situation?

RESOURCE 19

Focus Questions
(For use in peer supervision meetings)

Choose the set of questions and the particular question in the set
that will be most helpful to assess and develop the presenting
person's ministry. What will get at the crucial issue or situation?

A. Focus on the relationship between the group leader and group
1. Describe the relationship between you and the group.
   a. What are the strongest and most rewarding aspects?
   b. What aspects need improvement?
2. Do either you or your group get frustrated because of inap-
   propriate expectations?
   a. Expectations you place on the group or yourself.
   b. Expectations the group places on you or themselves.
   c. How are these expectations communicated?
3. Is your focus on process or results?
   a. How often do you offer solutions, give advice, or rescue
      group members?
   b. In what ways do you pressure yourself to make things
      happen?
   c. In what ways do you pressure group members to
      change their thinking or behavior?

B. Focus on spiritual concerns
1. What faith issues (purpose in life, sin, salvation, justice)
   seem important to you? To your group members?
2. How would you like to see God's presence become real in
   your relationships to the group?
   a. Have you encountered Jesus in your group members?
      How?
   b. Have your group members encountered Jesus in you?
      How?
3. How appropriate and effective are your use of traditional
   Christian resources?

a. How do you use the Bible?
b. How do you experience prayer?
c. How do you bestow a blessing on your group members?

C. Focus on feelings, skills, and role of the leader
1. Do the values, beliefs, or mannerisms of your group frustrate you?
   a. Do you take responsibility for your feelings toward the group?
   b. Can you appropriately express your feelings to the group? To us?
   c. How are your feelings helping or hindering your ministry to the group?
2. How are you doing as a Care Group leader?
   a. How well are you able to listen? Give examples.
   b. How well are you able to facilitate dialogue?
   c. How assertive are you with your group? Give examples.

D. Focus on problems in the group
1. What are your group members' problems as you see them? What do they think they are?
2. Do any aspects of your group members' situations seem too great for you to handle? If so, which ones? How do you plan to address these needs?
3. What is confusing about how your group or group members function? Can you give us background?
4. Have there been specific problems with loyalty, confidentiality, or availability?

RESOURCE 20

Possible Themes for Continuing Education
(For use by group leaders
in peer supervision meetings)

These themes assume that the thirteen topics in *Called to Care* have been covered. You may want to return to study some of those themes in greater depth.

Following are fifteen topics for possible study in continuing education. What concerns have you faced in your Care Group that are not listed? Nominate them for addition to the list. Then prioritize the list by indicating the six that you believe are most important.

_____ 1. Feelings—yours, mine and ours.
_____ 2. The art of listening
_____ 3. Counseling by telephone
_____ 4. Being appropriately assertive
_____ 5. Confidentiality
_____ 6. Using community resources
_____ 7. Hospital visitation
_____ 8. Ministering to those experiencing grief
_____ 9. Ministering to the dying
_____10. Ministering to depressed persons
_____11. Ministering to suicidal persons
_____12. Ministering to older persons
_____13. Ministering to those experiencing divorce
_____14. Ministering to inactive members
_____15. Ministering to new parents
_____16.
_____17.
_____18.
_____19.
_____20.

RESOURCE 21

Schedule for Supervisory/Continuing Education Meetings
(For use by pastor or overall coordinator and group leaders to plan schedule)

Indicate proposed dates for your monthly or semi-monthly meetings. Then indicate whose ministry will receive the in-depth supervision at that meeting. Also write in the continuing education themes as they are scheduled.

Date	In-depth Supervision	Continuing Education

RESOURCE 22

Evaluation of Supervisory Sessions
(To be used once or twice per year
by supervisory groups)

Rate the performance of your supervisory group in each of the following areas with an X on the line at the appropriate place. When finished, give the questionnaire to your leader. It will be tabulated and discussed at next month's meeting.

1. How did you feel about today's supervision session?

Great					Good					Terrible
10	9	8	7	6	5	4	3	2	1	0

2. Rate the distinctively Christian focus of your group.

Completely centered on Christ								Not at all centered on Christ		
10	9	8	7	6	5	4	3	2	1	0

3. How well focused was your supervision group during this session?

Tightly focused—We understood what we needed to do and did it.							Very unfocused—We were uncertain about our task and accomplished very little.			
10	9	8	7	6	5	4	3	2	1	0

4. How do you rate the tempo of the group in this session?

_____ Too fast

Just right   _____ Too slow

10	9	8	7	6	5	4	3	2	1	0

5. Share comments or suggestions that could improve the supervisory sessions.

7 Affirming Leaders

How Much Time Will You Give Them?

Jesus gave more time to his twelve disciples than to all of the rest of the world put together.[15] Giving time to someone is the key way of showing that person that you care. Someone has said that the word "love" can be spelled T-I-M-E.

As pastor, you will do well to give more time to your pastoral team members than you give to anybody else in the church. Often pastors spend most of their discretionary time ministering to new Christians or to problem-oriented people at the fringes of the church. To have an effective team, you need to shift time from actually doing that kind of ministry work, however important, to nurturing your ministry team.

Ways and occasions for giving time to your Care Group leaders might include:

1. At the beginning, when you recruit or interview potential leaders, give ample time. Be genuinely concerned about their well-being, use of strengths, and hopes and dreams for the future. Learn all you can about the future leaders!

2. As you conduct the training, show special interest in each person. In a very special way, you are a pastor to this team. Lis-

ten carefully, dialogue freely, and care deeply. Be there immediately if a Care Group leader faces a tragedy or crisis. You want your Care Group leaders to do unto others, their groups, as you have done to them. You are able to love your Care Group leaders because God and someone else first loved you. Keep the chain going!

3. Give undivided attention to all Care Group leaders as they give check-in reports. Empathize with a leader who expresses feelings about how things are going in his or her life or group. Make notes. Follow up on concerns you were not able to deal with in the group.

4. Once a year build a memory by doing something unusual with your Care Group leaders. Go white-water rafting together. Play basketball or golf. Visit a church where some outstanding ministry is happening. At a minimum, have a picnic or retreat where you can spend time simply *being* together in contrast to working together. If you spend quality time together, your relationships will grow deep and meaningful.

One caution. Even while you focus attention on the Care Group leaders, do not neglect taking time for your own relationship with God, with your partner, and family. The four great "P's" of priority are that you are first of all a **person** before God, then a **partner** to your spouse, a **parent** to your child (if these apply), and finally a **pastor** to your people. Model proper priorities for your Care Group leaders!

What Will Be the Satisfactions?

Relationships give meaning and satisfaction to life! Build strong relationships with your team members. Affirm and applaud the relationships they are building with their group members.

Satisfaction also comes from ministry. When your group leaders see their members overcome problems, when they see them establish relationships with God, or observe them blooming in a new way, their satisfaction level will increase.

A third satisfaction comes from a sense of belonging. All people need to feel they are part of a group and honestly needed by the group. Satisfaction will come when your group leaders feel they belong and are needed both by you on the pastoral team and by their group members. All need to feel that their ideas have had a fair hearing, that they have participated in making the rules, and that they are jointly making progress toward the goals they have set.

What Recognition Will Leaders Receive?

Good service needs to be recognized. Recognizing and affirming faithful servants builds standards. It sets up models and encourages others to aspire to God's kind of greatness. To avoid pride, focus on what has been done rather than on persons or personalities.

At a commissioning service, when the Care Group leaders have finished their training and are ready to begin leading a group, give affirmation for willingness. Commissioning is like a combined commencement and installation service. It offers an opportunity to report to the congregation what has been studied and what the person is willing to do.

Care Group meetings are the most important meetings of the church, or at least as important as any other. Each week announce the meetings and leaders in the church bulletin (see Resource 14 as a sample). A poster in the vestibule listing the Care Groups and picturing each Care Group leader is an appropriate way to give recognition to this important ministry of the church.

In pastoral reports it will be appropriate to express appreciation for the work done by the pastoral team. Include each Care Group leader's name in the report. Picture them when you print a church brochure.

In May or June affirm a year of faithful work with an expression of appreciation. You may want to encourage someone in each Care Group to lead in affirming their leader for what he or she has done or been to them. A special cake, or a card signed by all, might be appropriate. Be creative. If the person is in need, the group might want to take up a love offering. A turkey at Christmas or a meal out can add much celebration and joy to work that has been well done. Nothing will wear down a worker faster than lack of encouragement and affirmation from a supervisor.

A prayer of thanks in a worship service for what God has done through these servants can be an appropriate conclusion to the year. Honest words of appreciation will pay rich dividends in willingness to continue that which a leader has begun to do.

A Concluding Word to Pastors

The challenge of being a pastor to a group of lay pastors is not small. If you try it, you need to be warmly affirmed! One may hope you will receive your ultimate affirmation from God who modeled team building in Jesus Christ.

It is a common saying that "it is lonely at the top." All too often pastors find that to be true. The good news is that relief from loneliness can come by being a servant to a group of servants. That is what this concept of building a team of Care Group leaders has been about.

May the Spirit dwell in you richly, filling you with joy and peace and courage for all your endeavors in the Lord's service!

Notes

1. Robert E. Coleman, *The Master Plan of Evangelism* (Old Tappan, N.J.: Spire Books, 1963).

2. Dale Galloway, *20/20 Vision* (Portland, Ore.: Scott Publishing Company, 1988).

3. Paul Yonggi Cho, *Successful Home Cell Groups* (South Plainfield, N.J.: Bridge Publishing, 1981).

4. John Mallison, *Building Small Groups in the Christian Community* (West Ryde, Australia: Renewal Publications, 1978), p. 71.

5. Peter Wiwcharuck, *Building Effective Leadership* (Three Hills, Alberta: International Christian Leadership Development Foundation, Inc., 1987), p. 43.

6. Ibid. p. 43.

7. Exodus 18:13-26.

8. Lyman Coleman, *Prologue to Growth by Groups* (The Halfway House, Box 2, Newtown, Pa., p. 3).

9. See Wiwcharuck, p. 15.

10. Ibid., p. 268.

11. Based on "A Rite for Commissioning Stephen Ministers." Used by permission.

12. Kennon L. Callahan, *Twelve Keys to an Effective Church* (San Francisco: Harper & Row, 1983), p. 37.

13. Steve Barker, *Small Group Leaders' Handbook* (Downers Gove, Ill.: InterVarsity Press, 1982), p. 23.

14. Stephen Ministries, based in St. Louis, Missouri, has trained lay persons from over three thousand congregations to serve as lay caregivers.

15. See Robert E. Coleman, op. cit., chapter two.

The Author

Palmer Becker was born near Dolton, South Dakota, and raised on a dairy farm near Marion. He received his education from Freeman (S.D.) Junior College, Goshen (Ind.) College, and Mennonite Biblical Seminary (Elkhart, Ind.). He is currently a D.Min. candidate at Fuller Theological Seminary (Pasadena) where he is working on a catechism for the Mennonite churches called *Focusing Your Life*.

During the 1970s, Becker was called to lead the home mission and service ministries of the General Conference Mennonite Church. Under the banner of Living, Active Congregations, he promoted small groups and congregational outreach ministries throughout North America. During the 1980s, he was involved in church planting and university ministries work in Vancouver, B.C.

Becker is now lead pastor of the Bethel Mennonite Church in Mountain Lake, Minnesota. He is also consultant and field trainer for the Living in Faithful Evangelism (LIFE) program of the Mennonite and General Conference Mennonite churches. He and his wife, Ardys, are available for workshops and seminars on small groups.

Palmer and Ardys (Preheim) Becker are parents of four grown children—Byron (Kitchener, Ont.), Jo (Spring Valley, N.Y.), Sharla (Richmond, B.C.), and Steve (Costa Mesa, Calif.).